Study Guide

BUSINESS LAW

WITH UCC APPLICATIONS

Eighth Edition

Gordon W. Brown, J.D.
Member of the Massachusetts Bar
Professor of Law
North Shore Community College
Beverly, Massachusetts

Paul A. Sukys, J.D.
Member of the Ohio Bar
Professor of Law and Legal Studies
North Central Technical College
Mansfield, Ohio

GLENCOE
McGraw-Hill

New York, New York
Columbus, Ohio
Mission Hills, California
Peoria, Illinois

Study Guide—Business Law with UCC Applications, Eighth Edition

Imprint 1995
Copyright © 1993 by Glencoe/McGraw-Hill. All rights reserved. Copyright © 1989, 1983, 1978, 1972, 1966, 1961 by McGraw-Hill, Inc. All rights reserved. Copyright 1953 by McGraw-Hill, Inc. All rights reserved. Printed in the United States of America. Except as permitted under the United States Copyright Act, no part of this publication may be reproduced or distributed in any form or by any means, or stored in a database or retrieval system, without the prior written permission from the publisher. Previously published under the title *Individualized Performance Guide for College Business Law*. Send all inquiries to: Glencoe/McGraw-Hill, 936 Eastwind Drive, Westerville, Ohio 43081.

4 5 6 7 8 9 10   MAL   00 99 98 97 96 95

Contents

To the Student

This study guide is a student support supplement to the Eighth Edition of *Business Law with UCC Applications*. It provides a variety of involvement and application exercises to assist you in achieving the objectives of this course of study. Each chapter in this workbook can be completed successfully in formal class sessions; with an instructor who serves as a facilitator, consultant, or general resource person; or in independent study.

Before you begin to use this guide, you should familiarize yourself with its basic features. You will note that each chapter begins with a fill-in "Outline," followed by a "Legal Concepts" activity, a "Language of the Law" vocabulary review, and an "Applying the Law" series of case problems. Each of these activities has independent instructional value. However, used together, they can make it easier for you to succeed in achieving the goals of this course. Consistent and systematic review and study of the text in conjunction with the activities in this guide may also help to improve your scores on tests and examinations.

Completing this study guide is an answer key to the "Legal Concepts" and "Language of the Law" activities. It is recommended that you attempt to answer all exercises before referring to the answer key for confirmation of your responses. Answers to "Applying the Law" activities are included in the instructor's *Lecture Outline Book*.

The fill-in "Outline," which begins each chapter, offers a summary of the major points covered in that chapter. This outline correlates to the outline presented in each chapter opener in the text and may be used as a study aid or as an indicator of subject mastery. Answers are not provided for this activity. If you cannot fill in a blank, use your text to locate the appropriate response. Although this activity is suggested for each chapter of the text covered, its completion is *not* a substitute for a thorough reading and review of that chapter.

The "Legal Concepts" exercises are true-false statements designed to gauge your understanding of the concepts and principles introduced in the text. Completion of this activity will enable you to diagnose your strengths and weaknesses in mastering important concepts of law and help point out subject areas and topics presented in the text that require your further study.

"Language of the Law" is an activity that will help you to develop a working knowledge and understanding of key legal terms presented in the text. Strengthening your vocabulary will help you become more conversant and confident in classroom discussions concerning business law topics. This activity will also assist you in becoming familiar with, and retaining a comprehension of, terms you may encounter in your future business and legal relationships.

"Applying the Law" enables you to make immediate use, through interpretation and analysis, of principles learned in the text. You will find these cases ideally suited for classroom discussion because they are open to differing interpretations and opinions. This will help you to recognize and appreciate the fact that the law is not ironclad but subject to varying interpretations and applications.

This study guide has been produced both to test your comprehension of terms and concepts covered in the *Business Law with UCC Applications* text and to provide you with a quick and easy means of reviewing important chapter material. We wish you the best of luck in your course of study.

Gordon W. Brown
Paul A. Sukys

1 Ethics and Law

Chapter Outline

1-1 Ethical and Legal Dilemmas

A. Morals involve *values that govern society's attitude toward right & wrong*

B. Ethics attempts *to develop values ought to be & formulating & applying rules to keep values*

1-2 Ethical Theories

A. Ethical relativism claims that *there are no constant & unchanging standards of right & wrong.*

B. Utilitarianism determines ethical values by focusing on *the consequences of an action. Greatest good for the greatest number of people.*

C. Rational ethics establishes *objective, logical, and relatively consistent. human beings are ^morally responsible for their actions*

1-3 The Relationship Between Law and Ethics

A. The law consists of *rules of conduct established by the government to maintain harmony, stability, predictability, & justice with society*

B. Ethical principles can tell us *how to conduct & ourselves.*

1-4 The Sources of the Law

A. A constitution is *the basic law of a nation or state.*

  1. The articles of the U.S. Constitution establish the federal government.

    a. Article I establishes *legislative branch. (Statute making)* ^Congress

    b. Article II gives *executive power to the president*

    c. Article III gives *judicial power to Supreme court & other courts established by congress*

  2. The amendments to the Constitution establish *the rights that belong to the people, fine tune Constitution to update provisions to meet changing socioeconomic structure*

  3. Each state adopts *its own constitution which establishes the state's government, sets principles to guide state gov in making state laws & conducting state business*

  4. The principle of constitutional supremacy means *the U.S. Constitution is the Supreme law of the land.*

B. Statutory law is *a law passed by legislature. (Federal, Congress & signed by President) (State, state legislatures)*

C. Courts make laws in three ways:

  1. *Common law & precedent*

  2. *interpretation of statutes*

  3. *judicial review*

D. Administrative law is *decrees & decisions of agencies (commerce, communication, Aviation, labor relations, & working conditions)*

Legal Concepts

For each statement, write T in the answer column if the statement is true or F if the statement is false.

1. Ethics and law seek a common goal.
2. The theory of ethical relativism claims that there are unchanging standards of right and wrong.
3. Rational ethics focuses on the consequences of an action.
4. The Golden Rule is a principle of utilitarianism.
5. The law is needed because people do not always follow ethical principles.
6. The law and ethics never conflict.
7. The U.S. Constitution is the supreme law of the land.
8. All states are required to adopt uniform laws.
9. The tradition of common law began in England.
10. The court cannot interpret a statute unless it is presented with a case that involves that statute.
11. The first ten amendments to the U.S. Constitution are called the Bill of Rights.
12. Persuasive precedent must be followed by a court.
13. The power of judicial review belongs to Congress.
14. Congress can create administrative regulations but the state legislatures cannot.
15. The Administrative Procedures Act was repealed in 1972.

1. T
2. F
3. F
4. F
5. T
6. F
7. T
8. F
9. T
10. T
11. T
12. F
13. F
14. F
15. F

Language of the Law

Select the legal term that best matches each definition.

a. administrative law
b. binding precedent
c. code
d. common law
e. constitution
f. constitutional law
g. ethical relativism
h. ethics
i. judicial review
j. law
k. moral absolutism
l. morals
m. statute
n. Uniform Commercial Code
o. utilitarianism

1. An ethical theory that claims that there are no constant and unchanging standards of right and wrong
2. The values that govern a society's attitude toward right and wrong
3. A set of rules established by the government to maintain harmony, stability, and justice
4. The basic law of a nation or state
5. A compilation of all the statutes of a particular state
6. The process of determining the constitutionality of a statute
7. A law passed by a legislature
8. A previous case that a particular court must follow
9. An ethical theory that determines right from wrong by considering the consequences of an action
10. The body of law generated by the administrative agencies

1. g
2. L
3. J
4. E
5. C
6. I
7. M
8. B
9. O
10. A

2

Applying the Law

1. Bernardi was sent to Spain by his company Naci Electronics, Inc., to arrange for the sale of several million dollars of electronic equipment to a Spanish computer firm. Before finalizing the deal, Bernardi was told that the Spanish executives expected to receive large bribes to sign their names to the contract. Bernardi agreed to pay the bribes, despite the fact that he would never do so if the deal were negotiated in the United States. Name and explain the ethical system that Bernardi appeared to use to make his decision.

_____

_____

2. Tuttle was asked to explain how a utilitarian would determine a utilitarian ethical stance with regard to the death penalty. Tuttle responded by saying that the first step was to state the action to be evaluated. He then offered the following statement, "Kill all murderers so that they are not allowed to kill again." According to the first step in the utilitarian process, what error did Tuttle make here? Explain.

_____

_____

3. Burch worked as an engineer for the National Strategic Electronics Corporation. In her capacity as an engineer, Burch discovered that the company was producing substandard electronic devices that it then sold overseas to unsuspecting developing nations. If Burch revealed this information, several American plants would shut down, and literally thousands of workers would be laid off, including herself. Despite this, Burch disclosed what she learned. Name and explain the ethical theory that Burch used in making her decision.

_____

_____

4. LaRue found an old shopping bag containing $550. LaRue, who was out of work and desperately in need of cash, turned the bag over to the police. When he was asked why he turned in the money, LaRue said that he did it because that's what he would want someone else to do if it were his money. Name and explain the ethical theory that LaRue used in making his decision.

_____

_____

5. While watching a public television show on ancient civilizations, Alonso learned that certain cultures would exile their people to the wilderness when they became too old and feeble to be productive. Alonso declared that such a practice was right. When asked why she believed that it was right, she replied that the greatest good for the entire community was met by eliminating individuals who were a burden to the community. Name and explain the ethical belief to which Alonso adhered.

_____

_____

_____

_____

6. Lawson was arrested under a local ordinance that made it a crime to hold a political meeting if the participants were not affiliated with either the Republican or the Democratic party. Lawson claimed that the U.S. Constitution forbid such a prohibition. He argued that it violated the First Amendment's guarantee of freedom of assembly. The sheriff argued that the local ordinance did not have to comply with constitutional principles. Was the sheriff correct? Explain your response.

_____

_____

_____

7. The Pierce Corporation, headquartered in Delaware, agreed to purchase several shipments of steel from the Viking Steel and Tube Company, located in West Virginia. When Viking decided not to deliver the steel after all, Pierce sued. Lawyers for Viking said that the law regarding commercial transactions in West Virginia was totally different from the law regarding commercial transactions in Delaware. Were the lawyers for Viking correct? Explain.

_____

_____

_____

8. Loeb was arrested under a Wyoming statute that made drug addiction a crime. At trial, Loeb claimed that such a statute was invalid. When the Supreme Court of California declared a similar California statute invalid, Loeb argued that this decision was a binding precedent that the trial judge in his case would have to follow. Was Loeb correct? Explain.

_____

_____

_____

9. A state statute held that it was illegal to make negative comments about public officials. *The Loudonville Star* printed a negative news story about the Loudonville police chief. The chief then had McFly, the editor of *The Star*, arrested under the authority of the statute. McFly argued that the statute conflicted with the U.S. Constitution. The chief argued that the conflict with the U.S. Constitution did not matter as long as the statute was in line with the state constitution. Was the chief correct? Explain.

_____

_____

_____

10. Taylor owned a trucking firm that was involved in shipping goods throughout the country. He was told that a new regulation was about to be issued by the Interstate Commerce Commission (ICC) that might require him to make some rate changes. After the regulation went into effect, Taylor refused to comply. He argued that the ICC had too much power and that Congress had done nothing to curb that power or to prevent potential conflicts of interest. Was Taylor correct? Explain.

_____

_____

_____

2 Emerging Legal and Ethical Problems

Chapter Outline

2-1 Problems Involving Chemical Dependency

A. Alcohol abuse
   1. A merchant convicted of selling an alcoholic beverage to someone underage may be _____

   2. A sobriety checkpoint is defined as _____
_____

B. Drug abuse
   1. The Federal Controlled Substances Act categorizes drugs on the basis of _____
_____

   2. The Drug-Free Workplace Act is aimed at _____
_____

2-2 Problems Involving Property

A. Shoplifting is defined as _____
B. Vandalism is defined as _____

2-3 Problems Involving Safety and Security

A. Health and safety in the workplace
   1. OSHA was created to _____
_____

   2. One objective of the Hazard Communication Standard is _____
_____

   3. Under regulations established by OSHA, businesses must keep records of _____
_____
_____

B. Terrorism and hijacking
   1. International terrorism is defined in _____
   2. Under the Federal Aviation Act, the penalty for aircraft piracy is _____
_____

2-4 Problems Involving Rights

A. The Right of Free Speech is guaranteed by _____
_____

B. The right to die involves a clash between _____
_____

C. Employee privacy rights are protected by _____
_____

D. Student privacy rights are protected by _____
_____

Legal Concepts

For each statement, write T *in the answer column if the statement is true or* F *if the statement is false.*

1. Sobriety checkpoints violate the Fourth Amendment.
2. The Uniform Controlled Substances Act has been adopted by all of the states.
3. The Drug-Free Workplace Act requires companies with federal contracts to compel all employees to submit to drug testing.
4. The act of stealing goods from a store is known as shoplifting.
5. Vandalism is also called criminal damaging.
6. Parents of vandals are never required to pay for damage done by their children.
7. Public policy requires the government to protect the public.
8. All businesses affecting interstate commerce are regulated by OSHA.
9. Under OSHA regulations, logs of injuries and illnesses must be kept for five years.
10. There are no state statutes that prohibit the carrying of concealed weapons aboard an aircraft.
11. The burning of an American flag is not constitutionally protected speech.
12. The right to privacy is found in the First Amendment.
13. The majority of the states have made living wills legal.
14. The Employee Polygraph Protection Act prohibits most employers from using lie detector tests.
15. Parents have the right to see the educational records of their children.

1. _____
2. _____
3. _____
4. _____
5. _____
6. _____
7. _____
8. _____
9. _____
10. _____
11. _____
12. _____
13. _____
14. _____
15. _____

Language of the Law

Select the legal term that best matches each definition.

a. addict
b. chemical abuse
c. chemical dependency
d. kingpin provision
e. sobriety checkpoint
f. drug trafficking
g. public policy
h. shoplifting
i. vandalism
j. parental liability laws
k. living will

1. A document in which individuals can indicate their desire not to be kept alive by artificial means if there is no hope of recovery
2. Laws that require the parents of vandals to pay for the damage done by their children
3. A statutory provision that allows very severe penalties for major drug dealers
4. A temporary roadblock set up by police to stop cars at random to check for drunk drivers
5. The doctrine that says that the government has the duty to protect the people
6. The use of drugs or alcohol to such an extent that a person's judgment is impaired or his or her physical body is harmed
7. The willful or malicious causing of damage to property
8. The act of stealing goods from a store
9. The unauthorized manufacture or distribution of any controlled substance
10. An individual who is dependent upon drugs

1. _____
2. _____
3. _____
4. _____
5. _____
6. _____
7. _____
8. _____
9. _____
10. _____

Applying the Law

1. Christie Evans, 16 years old, went with several friends to a bar in New York. She borrowed a driver's license from a 24-year-old girlfriend to prove her age, if necessary. The bartender did not ask her to show him any identification. Her purchase of hard liquor was observed by an undercover agent for the state liquor control board. When the agent asked for Evans's identification, she produced the borrowed driver's license. The agent could tell immediately that Evans did not match the physical description on the license. Later, she admitted her true age. What penalties did the bartender face?

_____

_____

2. Dennis McGraw, the owner of McGraw Plumbing, Inc., hosted an annual Fourth of July party for his employees at their plant. Alcoholic beverages were always a part of the celebration. The drinks were served by a professional bartender who was hired specifically for the occasion. One year, Sammy Erwin appeared to have had a bit too much to drink. McGraw noticed Erwin's condition. What ethical and legal responsibilities did McGraw have in relation to Erwin? Should he have allowed the bartender to serve Erwin another drink?

_____

_____

3. Gale Reasoner, a salesperson for Ingram Defense Contractors, Inc., entertained several clients at a restaurant until 2 A.M. On her way home, she was stopped by the police who had set up a sobriety checkpoint on the main street in downtown Hamilton. Reasoner was found to be intoxicated and was jailed for the evening. Reasoner argued that the sobriety checkpoint was unconstitutional because it violated the Fourth Amendment rule against unreasonable searches conducted without warrants and without probable cause. Was she correct? Explain.

_____

_____

4. Gary Youngston hosted a party for several of his friends. During the party he gave his guests cocaine. One of his guests was an agent for the Drug Enforcement Agency. Youngston was arrested for violating the Federal Controlled Substances Act. Youngston argued that he could not be prosecuted because he did not sell the cocaine but merely gave it away. Was he correct? Explain.

_____

_____

5. Carrie Aciero applied for a job as a security officer for the Holland Computer Corporation. Since security officers carry firearms, she was required to undergo a drug test. Aciero refused to undergo the test arguing that her privacy rights outweighed public need in this situation. Was she correct? Explain.

_____

_____

6. While in a bookstore, Craig Humeston put a magazine under his jacket and prepared to leave the store. The owner of the store, who had observed Humeston's activity on a hidden security camera, challenged Humeston. Was Humeston able to claim that he did not intend to steal the magazine? Explain.

_____

_____

_____

7. Harry Juleard was with a group of his friends one night who decided to get "even" with a teacher. They entered the teacher's empty home and broke several expensive, antique figurines. All of the students were identified by a neighbor and were arrested. Juleard claimed that he was not guilty since he had been left outside as a lookout. The arresting officer told him that he was just as guilty as the ones who actually did the damage. Was the officer correct? Explain.

_____

_____

_____

8. Carl Kowalski discovered that his employer, the Union-Hopkins Development Corporation, was storing some very dangerous chemicals in its research facility. Kowalski filed a complaint with the local OSHA office about the dangerous chemicals. The OSHA office scheduled an inspection of the U-H research complex. Kowalski was fired for filing the complaint. Could U-H legally discharge Kowalski solely for his report to OSHA? Explain.

_____

_____

_____

9. Oscar Variant and Fred Tupperman own a paint shop in Norwalk. On March 17, they received a shipment of a new corrosive acid. Along with the shipment, they received a material safety data sheet (MSDS) from Brookville Chemical, the manufacturer of the acid. What duties did Variant and Tupperman have under OSHA regulations?

_____

_____

_____

10. Archie Davies owned and operated the Tower City Cinema. One Sunday afternoon, he saw that some demonstrators had set up a table at the entrance of the cinema. On the table was a placard that read in bright red letters, "Stop the New Incinerator Station Now!" The demonstrators were also handing out handbills. This action violated a policy that stated that no one was allowed to distribute handbills in the cinema for any purpose. Davies ordered the security guards to eject the demonstrators. The guards complied. However, the demonstrators filed a lawsuit seeking an injunction to prevent Davies from denying them access to the cinema to hand out the handbills. They argued that Davies had deprived them of their freedom of speech. Were they correct? Explain.

_____

_____

_____

8

3 The Judicial Process

Chapter Outline

3-1 The Court System

A. Jurisdiction is _____
_____

B. The federal court system is authorized by _____
_____

   1. U.S. District Courts are courts of _____
_____

   2. The 13 U.S. Courts of Appeals include

      a. _____

      b. _____

      c. _____

   3. The U.S. Supreme Court is the court of final jurisdiction in all cases appealed
from _____
_____

C. The courts of each state are organized according to _____
_____

3-2 Alternatives to Litigation

A. Compromise is _____

B. Mediation is _____

C. Arbitration is _____

D. Mandatory arbitration is _____
_____

3-3 Litigation Procedure

A. A lawsuit begins when a plaintiff files a complaint against a defendant.

   1. A plaintiff is _____

   2. A defendant is _____

   3. A complaint is _____

B. In the next stage of a lawsuit, a copy of the _____ and a(n) _____
must be given to the defendant.

C. In the third stage of a lawsuit, the defendant has a certain period of time in which to
file a(n) _____

D. During the pretrial stage of a lawsuit, several activities can be carried out, including

   1. _____

   2. _____

   3. _____

E. After the jury has been selected and opening statements have been made, the next steps in a trial include

1. _____
2. _____
3. _____
4. _____
5. _____

Legal Concepts

For each statement, write T *in the answer column if the statement is true or* F *if the statement is false.*

Answer

1. A court's jurisdiction is usually limited with respect to territory and type of case.
2. Each state and territory in the United States has at least two U.S. District Courts.
3. U.S. District Courts have jurisdiction over cases involving federal law only.
4. The U.S. Supreme Court has appellate jurisdiction only.
5. As a general rule, a federal court hearing a diversity case will apply the law of the state in which the federal court is physically located.
6. Most states have state courts that are lower than the general jurisdiction courts.
7. Mediation and arbitration are the same thing.
8. Requiring mandatory arbitration does not violate a person's constitutional rights as long as the arbitration does not replace the right to a jury trial.
9. A complaint will always ask for money from the defendant.
10. The objective of discovery is to simplify the issues and to avoid unnecessary arguments and surprises at trial.
11. Prospective jurors may be rejected if they have a financial interest in the outcome of a trial.
12. The instructions are given to the jury by the bailiff.
13. Either party in a lawsuit may appeal a judgment if that party believes an error was made during trial that unfavorably influenced the verdict.
14. Appellate procedures are essentially the same as trial procedures.
15. In civil cases, if a judgment is not paid, the court can order the loser's property to be sold by the sheriff to satisfy the judgment.

1. _T_
2. _____
3. _____
4. _____
5. _____
6. _____
7. _F_
8. _____
9. _____
10. _____
11. _____
12. _____
13. _T_
14. _____
15. _____

Language of the Law

Select the legal term that best matches each definition.

a. answer
b. arbitration
c. complaint
d. defendant
e. discovery

f. diversity cases
g. general jurisdiction
h. mediation
i. original jurisdiction
j. plaintiff

k. service of process
l. special jurisdiction
m. summary judgment
n. writ of certiorari
o. writ of execution

Answer

1. A court's authority to hear a case when it is first brought to court
2. A court's authority to hear any type of case
3. An order to a lower court to deliver its records to the U.S. Supreme Court
4. The process by which a third party actually decides a dispute for two other parties
5. The person who brings a legal suit
6. Giving the complaint and summons to the defendant
7. The process by which a third party is invited to persuade contending parties to settle their dispute

1. _____
2. _____
3. _B_
4. _B_
5. _____
6. _____
7. _h_

8. A motion asking the court for an immediate decision in favor of the party making the motion

8. _____

9. The process by which the parties to a civil action search for information relevant to the case

9. _____

10. A court order giving the sheriff the power to satisfy a judgment by selling the property of the loser of a lawsuit

10. _____

Applying the Law

1. Morgan brought suit in federal district court against the Simpson Corporation alleging certain violations of federal antitrust laws. Along with these allegations, Morgan also accused Simpson of certain state contract law violations arising from the same situation that created the antitrust violations. Simpson argued that the state claims could not be handled by the federal court. Simpson was wrong. Why?

_____

_____

_____

2. Drake, a citizen of Vermont, was the subject of several outright lies in a book written and published by Kramer, a citizen of New Hampshire. Drake decided to sue Kramer in U.S. District Court in New Hampshire. Drake asked the court for $9,000 in damages for losses suffered as the result of Kramer's lies. Kramer argued that Drake could not sue him in federal court. Kramer was correct. Why?

_____

_____

_____

3. McCoy, a citizen of Maryland, was injured in a plane crash. McCoy sued the airline in federal court in Delaware, which was where the corporation had its headquarters. McCoy argued that the federal court should use the law of Rhode Island to decide the case, since that was where the plane had crashed. The airline argued that the court should use principles of general law to decide the case, rather than the law of any specific state. Both were incorrect. Why?

_____

_____

_____

4. Yates invented a new process for deadening sound. He had the process patented so that no one else could use it without his permission. Carson copied the process and began to market it under another name. Yates sued Carson in U.S. District Court and won the case. Carson appealed to the appropriate federal court of appeals and lost again. He now says that the U.S. Supreme Court must hear his case. Carson will not be able to do this. Why?

_____

_____

_____

5. Lewis was seriously injured when his physician, Dr. Ruggles, used an improper procedure during an operation. Lewis decided to sue Dr. Ruggles. Lewis was told that he must first submit the case to arbitration. Lewis argued that such mandatory arbitration was unconstitutional. Lewis was incorrect. Why?

_____

_____

6. Lucas and Saunders opened a restaurant in Jeromesville. After several of their customers suffered serious food poisoning, they found themselves facing a lawsuit. After being served with a complaint and summons, Lucas and Saunders contacted an attorney. They told the attorney that the food poisoning resulted from a shipment of spoiled fish that had been canned improperly. They wanted to bring the cannery into the lawsuit. How could this be done?

_____

_____

_____

7. Oliver was injured when a bridge collapsed in Butler County. He sued Butler County for not maintaining the bridge properly. During discovery, Oliver asked his attorney to have several key witnesses respond to a series of interrogatories. Oliver's attorney refused. Why?

_____

_____

_____

8. Gower was a prospective juror in a case involving a boating accident. While examining the jury prior to trial, the plaintiff's attorney found out that Gower owned a boat. Since the outcome of the trial might result in higher insurance rates for boat owners, the attorney asked that Gower be dismissed. The court refused to do so, despite Gower's financial interest. Why?

_____

_____

_____

9. Layfield witnessed a fistfight that eventually led to a lawsuit. When the plaintiff lost the case at trial, he appealed it to the intermediate appellate court. Layfield was afraid she'd have to testify again in front of the appeals court. Her fears were unfounded. Why?

_____

_____

_____

10. Culler sued Bradley after Bradley refused to honor a sales contract. When Bradley lost the case, he told Culler that he owned no property and could not pay the judgment from either his wages or his checking account. How could Culler compel Bradley to pay the judgment?

_____

_____

_____

4 Criminal Law

Chapter Outline

4-1 Definition and Classes of Crimes

A. A crime is _____

B. Criminal law in the American system

    1. Federal authority for the establishment of the FBI and other police agencies is found in _____

    2. State governments have inherent _____

C. Classes of crimes

    1. A felony is _____

    2. A misdemeanor is _____

D. Penalties for criminal offenses

    1. A fine is _____

    2. An indeterminate sentence is _____

    3. A determinate sentence is _____

    4. A mandatory sentence is _____

    5. Cruel and unusual punishment is prohibited by _____

4-2 Elements of a Crime

A. The two elements necessary to create criminal liability are _____

B. The four most commonly recognized mental states in criminal law are

    1. _____

    2. _____

    3. _____

    4. _____

C. In criminal law, motive is _____

4-3 Defenses to Criminal Liability

A. The three tests for determining the insanity of a defendant are

   1. _____

   2. _____

   3. _____

B. Entrapment occurs when _____

C. Self-defense is available to defendants if they can show

   1. _____

   2. _____

   3. _____

D. Defense of family members is a valid defense as long as _____

E. The battered spouse syndrome is a form of _____

F. Mistake is a defense to criminal liability if _____

4-4 Specific Crimes

A. Crimes against people include _____

B. Crimes against property include _____

C. Crimes involving business include _____

D. Computer crimes include _____

Legal Concepts

For each statement, write T *in the answer column if the statement is true or* F *if the statement is false.*

Answer

1. Crimes are punishable by the official governing body of a nation or state.   1. F

2. A misdemeanor is punishable by a jail term of six months or less.   2. F

3. The federal government has inherent police power.   3. _____

4. A determinate sentence requires a prisoner to spend a specified period of time incarcerated.   4. _____

5. The death penalty has been completely outlawed by the Supreme Court.   5. _____

6. The First Amendment prohibits cruel and unusual punishment.   6. F

7. Refusal to act can sometimes be considered criminal.   7. _____

8. Motive is an essential element of criminal liability.   8. _____

9. Recklessness requires a perverse disregard of a known risk.   9. _____

10. The oldest test of insanity is the M'Naghten Rule.   10. T

11. People found NGRI automatically go free.   11. _____

12. Defense of family members is a valid defense in most states.   12. T

13. Many courts consider the battered spouse syndrome defense to be a form of self-defense.   13. _____

14. The unlawful touching of another person is called battery.   14. _____

15. The crime of rape is limited to situations in which a male forces a female to have sexual intercourse.   15. _____

Language of the Law

Select the legal term that best matches each definition.

a. bribery   e. homicide   i. purpose
b. entrapment   f. irresistible impulse test   j. robbery
c. felony   g. larceny   k. self-defense
d. forgery   h. negligence

Answer

1. The false making or changing of a writing with the intent to defraud
2. Carrying away the property of another without the right to do so
3. To act with the intent to cause the result that does, in fact, occur
4. The act of taking personal property from the possession of another against that person's will
5. The use of force to protect oneself against death or serious injury
6. The insanity test that claims that as a result of mental disease the defendant did not know right from wrong or was compelled to commit the crime
7. To act without seeing the possible negative consequences of the action
8. The killing of one human being by another
9. A corrupt agreement induced by an offer of reward
10. A crime punishable by death or imprisonment for a term exceeding one year

1. _____
2. _____
3. _____
4. _____
5. _____
6. __*F*_____
7. _____
8. _____
9. _____
10. __*C*_____

Applying the Law

1. Conrad, a known fence, approached several people in the neighborhood offering to buy stolen property. Mr. Girard reported this behavior to the police. The police then sent an undercover officer to investigate. When Conrad attempted to purchase stolen goods allegedly in the possession of the undercover officer, the officer arrested him. Conrad claimed that he was the victim of entrapment. Was he correct? Explain.

_____

_____

_____

2. While walking in his neighborhood, Andy Ranier was approached by several young men who demanded money from him. When he refused, they attacked him. Ranier pulled out a gun and shot one of his attackers. Ranier was later charged with attempted murder. Ranier claimed he acted in self-defense. Was he correct? Explain.

_____

_____

_____

3. Georgette McArthur brought her car into the Parker Muffler Shop for a new exhaust system. The shop manager told McArthur that she could pick up the keys to her loaner car at the front desk. By mistake, McArthur took the keys to Claremount's Accord. When Claremount could not find his car, he called the police and reported it stolen. Did McArthur commit the criminal act of car theft? Explain.

_____

_____

_____

4. Jenkins's daughter was raped by Martinique. Martinique confessed to the charges and was given a suspended sentence. Jenkins was in the courtroom when this was announced. In a state of extreme rage, Jenkins killed Martinique. While Jenkins's actions were clearly intentional, they were performed in a state of extreme anger as a result of a reasonable provocation. What crime did Jenkins commit? Explain.

_____

_____

5. Craig Newton was angry at Fred Zimmerman because Zimmerman was promoted to the position that Newton believed was rightfully his. Newton waited for Zimmerman in a dark alley in back of the factory where they both worked. Mistaking Daniels for Zimmerman, Newton attacked and beat Ralph Daniels. Newton argued that he attacked Daniels by mistake and should not be held criminally liable. Was he correct? Explain.

_____

_____

6. Patricia Selan and George Wilson dated for seven months. One Friday evening, Patricia and George were watching television in her apartment. George became unusually aggressive with Patricia who repeatedly told him to stop. George, however, did not stop but became progressively violent until he forced Patricia to have sex with him. He claimed that because of their long-term relationship his action could not be considered rape. Was he correct? Explain.

_____

_____

7. While sleepwalking in his dormitory one night, Stevens ran into Claymore, a classmate. Stevens knocked Claymore down some stairs. Claymore wanted the police to arrest Stevens. Did the police comply with the request? Explain.

_____

_____

8. Morris offered the mayor of Shelby $10,000 to award Morris's firm a highway contract. The mayor refused the bribe. When Morris was arrested, he claimed that he was innocent of the charge of bribery because the mayor never took the money. Was he correct? Explain.

_____

_____

9. Schmitt took a shortcut through Woodward's backyard. While passing by Woodward's living room, he saw a valuable camera on a table. Schmitt opened a window and used a long stick to lift the camera by its strap and haul it out the window. When charged with burglary, Schmitt argued that he had neither broken into nor entered the Woodward home. Therefore, he concluded that he could not be charged with burglary. Was he correct? Explain.

_____

_____

10. Magill was cleaning his .45 automatic revolver when it discharged and killed his friend. Magill claimed that he could not be charged with any crime because the killing was unintentional. Was he correct? Explain.

_____

_____

5 Tort Law

Chapter Outline

5-1 Tort Law Defined

A. A tort is _____

B. The doctrine of *respondeat superior* may impose tort liability on _____

_____

C. A duty is _____

5-2 Intentional Torts

A. Assault and battery

    1. An assault occurs when _____

    2. A battery occurs when _____

B. False imprisonment is _____

C. Defamation is _____

    1. Libel is _____

    2. Slander is _____

    3. Actual malice requires _____

    4. Actual malice applies to _____

D. Invasion of privacy is _____

E. Misuse of legal procedure occurs when _____

F. To succeed, a lawsuit based on the intentional infliction of emotional distress must involve conduct that is _____

G. A nuisance is _____

H. Intentional interference with a contract occurs when _____

_____

5-3 Negligence

A. The elements of negligence are

    1. _____

    2. _____

    3. _____

    4. _____

B. Defenses to negligence include

    1. _____

    2. _____

    3. _____

5-4 Strict Liability

A. The doctrine of strict liability applies to ultrahazardous activities including

1. _____

2. _____

3. _____

B. Product liability extends to

1. _____

2. _____

3. _____

5-5 Remedies for Torts

A. The right to damages

1. Damages are _____

2. Punitive damages are _____

B. An injunction is _____

5-6 Tort Reform

A. Survival statutes allow _____

B. Wrongful death statutes preserve _____

C. A damage cap is _____

D. A federal tort reform act would _____

Legal Concepts

For statement, write T in the answer column if the statement is true or F if the statement is false.

Answer

1. A tort is a private wrong that injures another person's well-being, property, or reputation.
2. The primary purpose of tort law is to compensate the innocent victim.
3. Employers can never be held liable for the torts of their employees.
4. Assault and battery always occur together.
5. Libel is defamation in a temporary form.
6. The actual malice test applies only to public officials.
7. In general, only public authorities can begin a lawsuit for public nuisance.
8. The reasonable person test is a subjective test.
9. Proximate cause is not a necessary element of negligence.
10. Actual harm is a necessary element of negligence.
11. Comparative negligence completely prevents recovery by the injured party.
12. Assumption of the risk involves the voluntary exposure of the victim to a known risk.
13. Strict liability is generally applied when the harm that results comes from an ultrahazardous activity.
14. Damages cannot include compensation for lost wages.
15. The rights of third parties affected by the death of the deceased are preserved by survival statutes.

1. _____
2. _T_____
3. _F_____
4. _F_____
5. _____
6. _____
7. _____
8. _____
9. _____
10. _____
11. _____
12. _____
13. _____
14. _____
15. _____

Language of the Law

Select the legal term that best matches each definition.

a. assault
b. battery
c. damage cap
d. damages

e. defamation
f. injunction
g. false imprisonment
h. libel

i. nuisance
j. punitive damages
k. tort
l. tortfeasor

Answer

1. A person who commits a tort
2. Placing a victim in fear of immediate bodily harm
3. Damages designed to punish
4. An offensive, or harmful, unprivileged touching
5. Defamation of a permanent form
6. Preventing another party from moving about freely
7. Any false statement that harms another's good name or reputation
8. Anything that endangers life or health, offends the senses, violates the laws of decency, or prevents the reasonable or comfortable use of property
9. A court order preventing the performance of an act
10. An upper limit to the amount of damages that can be recovered

1. _____
2. _____
3. _J_____
4. _b_____
5. _h_____
6. _____
7. _E_____
8. _____
9. _____
10. _____

Applying the Law

1. Laura Mason, a waitress for the Highland Restaurant, was working in the dining room one morning when Fred VonStyne, a customer, said something that annoyed her. Without warning Mason approached VonStyne waving her tray menacingly. Before she could touch VonStyne she was restrained by another waitress. When she was sued by VonStyne for assault, she argued that she could not possibly have committed an assault because she never touched VonStyne. Was she correct? Explain.

_____

_____

2. Roy Taggart owned and operated the Taggart Dress Shop. Taggart thought he saw Violet Damron place a blouse in her shopping bag. Taggart apprehended Damron and locked her in a closet for six hours. When Taggart was satisfied that Damron was innocent, he released her. Damron sued for false imprisonment. Did she have a case? Explain.

_____

_____

3. Addie Franklin worked as a nurse at the Riverside County Clinic. Franklin read the records of Karen Gromley, another nurse who worked at the clinic. The records revealed that Gromley was in the hospital suffering from a very serious illness. Concerned about Gromley's health, Franklin spread the news of Gromley's illness throughout the clinic and took up a collection to buy flowers. When Gromley threatened an invasion of privacy suit, Franklin argued that because of her good motive in revealing Gromley's illness, the lawsuit would be groundless. Was she correct? Explain.

_____

_____

4. Willy Evans and Olaf Erickson did not get along as neighbors. Evans filed a false and groundless lawsuit against Erickson for defamation. The lawsuit was resolved in Erickson's favor. What type of lawsuit, if any, could Erickson now bring against Evans? Explain.

_____

_____

_____

5. Rick Gardner, the owner of a baseball stadium, was sued by Ted Fuller, a spectator who was injured by a foul ball hit during a game in Gardner's stadium. Gardner claimed that the lawsuit would not hold up as long as it could be shown that Fuller was aware of the risk of injuries from foul balls, which are associated with viewing baseball in a stadium. Was he correct? Explain.

_____

_____

_____

6. While test driving her new motorcycle on an interstate highway, Giordano decided to take the bike up to 110 miles per hour and try several tricky maneuvers in heavy traffic. As a result, she lost control of the bike and crashed into several automobiles and trucks, injured several people, and caused extensive damage to the vehicles. Giordano was sued by the victims. What test was used to judge her conduct to determine whether she breached her duty to the other people on the interstate? Explain.

_____

_____

_____

7. Charlene Wilkinson purchased a hairdryer from Frederickson's Appliance Store. That afternoon she plugged it in and received a severe shock for which she was briefly hospitalized. An investigation revealed that the entire line of hairdryers had been manufactured based on a defective wiring diagram. Wilkinson sued the manufacturer, Milligan Electronics, Inc., and the seller, Frederickson's Appliance Store. Wilkinson argued that the hairdryer had been sold to her in a defective condition. Name and explain the legal theory that she was using.

_____

_____

_____

8. Abrams recklessly drove his snowmobile down several city streets during a snowstorm. While doing so he failed to see several pedestrians crossing the street and collided with them, injuring them seriously. Abrams argued that he had no duty to avoid hitting pedestrians who are in the street during a snowstorm. Was he correct? Explain.

_____

_____

_____

9. Baker was playing with a neighbor's hunting rifle when it discharged accidentally. The bullet from the rifle hit Baker's front lawn, causing no damage to anyone or to the property. Baker said that he was not negligent in this incident. Was he correct? Explain.

_____

_____

_____

10. Beatty invited Parsons on a boat ride out in Lake Erie. After several hours, Parsons told Beatty that she wanted to return to shore. Beatty refused and, despite continued protests from Parsons, kept her on the water for five more hours. Parsons sued Beatty for false imprisonment. Beatty argued that there was no false imprisonment because Parsons was not restrained or locked up. Was he correct? Explain.

_____

_____

_____

6 The Nature, Characteristics, and Status of Contracts

Chapter Outline

6-1 The Nature of Contracts

A. A contract is _____

B. The six elements of a contract are

   1. _____

   2. _____

   3. _____

   4. _____

   5. _____

   6. _____

C. Privity means _____

6-2 Contractual Characteristics

A. Valid, void, voidable, and unenforceable contracts

   1. A valid contract is _____

   2. A void contract is _____

   3. A voidable contract is _____

   4. An unenforceable contract is _____

B. Unilateral and bilateral contracts

   1. A unilateral contract is _____

   2. A bilateral contract is _____

C. Express and implied contracts

   1. An express contract is _____

   2. An implied-in-fact contract is _____

   3. An implied-in-law contract is _____

D. Informal and formal contracts

    1. An informal contract is _____

_____

    2. A formal contract is _____

_____

    3. A contract of record is _____

_____

6-3 Status of Contracts   **A.** An executory contract is _____

_____

    B. An executed contract is _____

_____

Legal Concepts

For each statement, write T *in the answer column if the statement is true or* F *if the statement is false.*

Answer

1. All contracts must be in writing to be enforceable.
    1. _F_____
2. A legally complete contract arises between two parties when at least four of the six elements of a contract are present.
    2. _____
3. Article 2 of the Uniform Commercial Code (UCC) sets down the rules that govern sale of goods contracts.
    3. _____
4. A general rule of contract law is that the parties to a contract must stand in privity to one another.
    4. _____
5. All contracts contain agreements but not all agreements are contracts.
    5. _T_____
6. A voidable contract has no legal effect whatsoever.
    6. _____
7. An unenforceable contract may have all of the elements of a complete contract and still may not be upheld by a court of law.
    7. _T_____
8. A unilateral contract comes into existence at the moment the initial promise is made.
    8. _____
9. An express contract is created by the actions or gestures of the parties involved in the transaction.
    9. _____
10. The quasi-contract concept cannot be applied when one party bestows a benefit on another party unnecessarily or through misconduct or negligence.
    10. _____
11. Any oral or written contract that is neither under seal nor a contract of record is considered an informal contract.
    11. _____
12. A formal contract differs from other contracts in that it has to be written, signed, witnessed, placed under the seal of the parties, and delivered.
    12. _____
13. All states still require the use of the seal in agreements related to the sale of real property.
    13. _____
14. Contracts of record are not true contracts because they are court created.
    14. _____
15. A contract can never be partly executory.
    15. _F_____

Language of the Law

Select the legal term that best matches each definition.

a. bilateral contract
b. breach of contract
c. contract
d. contract of record
e. executed contract

f. executory contract
g. express contract
h. implied-in-fact contract
i. implied-in-law contract
j. privity

k. unenforceable contract
l. unilateral contract
m. valid contract
n. voidable contract
o. void contract

Answer

1. A special type of formal contract having certain unique characteristics
   1. _____

2. A contract that can be imposed by a court in a situation in which it can be proved that the parties did not create a written, oral, or implied-in-fact agreement
   2. _____

3. A contract that has not yet been fully performed
   3. *F* _____

4. An agreement between two or more competent parties, based on mutual promises to do or to refrain from doing some particular thing that is neither illegal nor impossible
   4. _____

5. A condition that exists when both parties to a contract have a legally recognized interest in the subject of the contract
   5. _____

6. A contract, the terms of which have been completely and satisfactorily carried out by both parties
   6. _____

7. A contract that is legally binding and fully enforceable
   7. _____

8. A contract in which both parties make promises
   8. _____

9. The failure of one of the parties to a contract to do what he or she has previously agreed to do
   9. _____

10. A contract that can be canceled by one of the parties
    10. *N* _____

Applying the Law

1. Abbott and Sayers entered into a contract whereby Sayers agreed to purchase a tract of land owned by Abbott. Later, when a dispute arose as to the interpretation of certain contractual terms, Abbott argued that they should consult Article 2 of the UCC. Explain what is wrong with Abbott's advice.

_____

_____

_____

2. The American Organization of Communication Consultants (AOCC) entered into a contract with the Silverton City Convention Bureau to hold the AOCC's annual convention at the Silverton City Convention Center. Later the AOCC breached the agreement and moved the convention to Bellaire. Holland, who owned the Holland Tea House, a restaurant directly across the street from the Silverton Convention Center, sued the AOCC for breach of contract. His suit failed. Why?

_____

_____

_____

3. Woo, a minor, entered into a contract with Laumer, an adult, for the purchase of a painting. Later, Woo decided she did not like the painting and tried to return it to Laumer. Laumer refused to accept the painting or to return Woo's money, arguing that the contract was completely valid and that Woo had no right to change her mind and cancel the agreement. Laumer was incorrect. Why?

_____

_____

4. Adams lost an expensive ring. He placed an ad in the local newspaper offering a $50 reward for the return of the ring. Parker read the ad and spent two days looking for it. Although she did not find the ring, she still went to Adams's home the next day and asked for the $50. Adams correctly refused to pay Parker. Why?

_____

_____

_____

5. Harper watched as a landscape crew spent an entire day planting new bushes and trees in her front lawn, reseeding her lawn, and treating her flower beds with chemicals. When presented with a bill, Harper refused to pay, claiming she had not ordered the service. When the crew rechecked their work order, they found out they were on the wrong block. Harper will have to pay for the work anyway. Explain why.

_____

_____

_____

6. Adler took his car to the E-Z Car Wash Company and arranged to have the car washed. Through a mix-up in the paperwork, Adler's car was washed and waxed. When Adler returned, he refused to pay for the wax job. E-Z argued that a court would force Adler to pay under the principle of quasi-contract. E-Z was incorrect. Why?

_____

_____

_____

7. Carson and Forbes entered into an agreement in which Carson agreed to sell his VCR to Forbes. The two parties wrote all the terms of the contract on the back of an old envelope. They then both signed the agreement. When the time came to execute the contract, Forbes claimed he was not bound by the terms because the law required all contracts to be formally drawn up on pre-printed documents. He was incorrect. Why?

_____

_____

_____

8. Hume agreed to take his two younger brothers to the Super Bowl. When the time came to go to the game, Hume discovered that all the tickets had been sold two weeks prior to his original agreement with his brothers. When Hume told them that he could not get tickets, they told him that they were going to sue him. Hume told his brothers they could not sue him for failing to obtain the tickets. He was correct. Why?

_____

_____

_____

9. Watson promised to sell his guitar to Coates if Coates would give him $250 in return. Coates promised to bring the money to Watson in exchange for the guitar. When Coates showed up with the money the next day, Watson refused to turn over the guitar, arguing that promises alone, without action, cannot create a contract. Watson was incorrect. Why?

_____

_____

_____

10. Austin agreed to construct a restaurant for Dewey. Before construction began, a change in the zoning regulations made it illegal to open a restaurant on Dewey's property. Austin argued that the contract was still valid. He was incorrect. Why?

_____

_____

_____

7 Offer and Acceptance

Chapter Outline

7-1 Requirements of an Offer

A. An offer is _____

B. An offer is invalid if it is made _____

_____

C. To be definite, an offer should identify

  1. _____

  2. _____

  3. _____

  4. _____

7-2 Acceptance of an Offer

A. Communication of acceptance may be express or implied.

  1. In face-to-face dealings, acceptance is complete when _____

  2. If acceptance is made through the same medium that the offer is made through, acceptance is complete when _____

_____

  3. When the offeree selects a medium different from the one used by the offeror, acceptance is complete when _____

_____

B. To be effective, an acceptance must be unequivocal.

  1. The mirror image rule says _____

  2. Under the Uniform Commercial Code (UCC), if the parties are not merchants, new terms are to be construed as _____

_____

  3. Under the UCC, if the parties are both merchants, new terms become part of the agreement unless

    a. _____

    b. _____

7-3 Rejection of an Offer

A rejection comes about when _____

_____

7-4 Revocation of an Offer

Offers may be revoked by

A. _____

B. _____

C. _____

D. _____

E. _____

F. _____

A. An option contract is _____

_____

B. Under the UCC, a firm offer is _____

_____

Legal Concepts

For each statement, write T *in the answer column if the statement is true or* F *if the statement is false.*

Answer

1. An offer made as an obvious joke is invalid.   1. _____
2. Most courts require absolute definiteness of terms before validating an offer.   2. _____
3. The UCC forbids the omission of any information in an offer.   3. _____
4. An offer must be communicated to the offeree in order to be valid.   4. _____
5. Newspaper and magazine advertisements are always considered public offers.   5. _____
6. Bilateral contracts do not usually require communication of an expressed acceptance.   6. _____
7. Communication of acceptance of an offer must always be express.   7. _____
8. An offer made by telegram and accepted by telegram becomes effective when the acceptance is received by the offeror.   8. _____
9. If an acceptance changes or qualifies the terms in the offer, it is not an acceptance.   9. _____
10. The UCC has altered the mirror image rule.   10. _____
11. The delivery of unordered merchandise through the mail is now considered an offer to sell.   11. *T*
12. An offeree can force an offeror into a contract by remaining silent if the offeror initiated the silence condition.   12. _____
13. When no time limit is set, an offer remains open until it is expressly revoked by the offeror.   13. *F*
14. Destruction of the subject matter related to an offer automatically revokes that offer.   14. *T*
15. The UCC requires consideration when a merchant agrees in writing to hold an offer open.   15. _____

Language of the Law

Select the legal term that best matches each definition.

a. acceptance
b. cost-plus contract
c. current market price contract
d. firm offer
e. invitation to trade

f. mirror image rule
g. offer
h. offeree
i. offeror
j. option contract

k. output contract
l. public offer
m. rejection
n. requirements contract
o. revocation

Answer

1. An agreement that binds an offeror to a promise to hold an offer open for a predetermined or a reasonable length of time   1. *J*
2. A proposal by one party to another indicating a willingness to enter into a contract   2. _____
3. An agreement in which prices of certain goods are determined by reference to the market price of the goods as of a specified date   3. _____
4. A contract in which one party agrees to sell to a second party all the goods that the first party makes in a given period of time   4. _____
5. The person to whom an offer is made   5. _____

6. An announcement published to reach many people for the purpose of creating interest and attracting responses

6. _____

7. The legal doctrine that holds that the terms in an acceptance must be identical to the terms of the offer

7. *F* _____

8. The calling back of an offer by the offeror

8. *O* _____

9. An offer made through the public media but intended for a specific person whose identity or address is unknown

9. _____

10. The person who makes an offer

10. _____

Applying the Law

1. Cabot awoke one morning to find that his water pipes were not working. After some investigation, he discovered that the water main leading to his house had broken. The plumber told him it would cost $600 to repair the damage. At this point, Cabot told the plumber he'd gladly sell the whole house for $600 just to be rid of it. The plumber was not entitled to consider this statement a valid offer. Why not?

_____

_____

2. Walker sent a letter to Pike which stated, "I'd like to purchase one of your antique cars for between $25,000 and $27,000." Pike would not be entitled to consider this letter a valid offer. Why not?

_____

_____

3. When McCarthy rented her apartment from Corbett, he offered to pay a fair share of the costs for redecorating several rooms. After the redecorating was done, Corbett refused to reimburse McCarthy for any of the expenses. What error did McCarthy make in her initial negotiation with Corbett?

_____

_____

4. Riley found a purse at the local shopping mall. By looking in the purse, Riley determined that it belonged to Watson. When he delivered the purse to Watson, she thanked him but did nothing more. The next day, Riley found out that Watson had posted a notice at the mall offering $50 for the return of the purse. When he asked Watson for the reward, she refused to give it to him. Watson was correct in her refusal. Why?

_____

_____

5. Simons sent a telegram to Hatcher offering to purchase Hatcher's hunting lodge for $100,000. Hatcher decided to sell the lodge and sent a letter to Simons stating his decision. Before receiving the letter, Simons purchased another hunting lodge owned by Edwards. Hatcher claimed that Simons must also buy Hatcher's lodge because Simons's acceptance was valid when Hatcher mailed the letter. Hatcher was incorrect. Why?

_____

_____

_____

6. The president of Rader Industries offered Kubach a job as human resources director. Kubach said she would take the job as long as the president agreed to grant her an annual $1,500 bonus each Christmas. The president refused to agree to the bonus. Kubach argued that the president had to agree because Kubach had already accepted the president's offer and had thus created a contract. Kubach was incorrect. Why?

_____

_____

_____

7. Ludwig watched all day long as contractors from the Frazetta Cement Company laid a new driveway on his property. The contractors were actually at the wrong house and on the wrong street. When Frazetta later billed Ludwig, he refused to pay. Ludwig was incorrect in this refusal. Why?

_____

_____

_____

8. Knight received a set of bathroom towels through the mail from a merchandising house in Casper, Wyoming. A letter sent with the towels told her she could either send the merchandising house $20 or return the set within 14 days. Knight did neither. Instead, she kept the towels and used them in her bathroom. Knight was correct in keeping the towels. Explain.

_____

_____

_____

9. Russell wanted to sell several acres of land he owned near Rattlesnake Cliffs. He wrote a letter to Flenner stating in part, "If I don't receive an answer from you by noon on February 28, I will take your silence as an acceptance." Flenner did not respond by noon on February 28. Flenner now has the right to hold Russell to the agreement. Why?

_____

_____

_____

10. Massie offered to sell Claypool some lakeshore property for $67,000. Claypool asked for time to consider the offer. Massie agreed to hold the offer open for one week in return for Claypool's payment of $25. The next day, Claypool told Massie that he had decided not to purchase the property. Claypool then asked for his money back. Massie refused to return the $25. Massie's refusal was correct. Why?

_____

_____

_____

28

8 Mutual Assent and Defective Agreement

Chapter Outline

8-1 Mutual Assent

    A. Mutual assent means _____

    _____

    B. A defective agreement can result from _____

    _____

8-2 Fraud and Misrepresentation

    A. To sue for fraud, the complaining party must prove

        1. _____

        2. _____

        3. _____

        4. _____

        5. _____

    B. Active fraud occurs when _____

    _____

    C. Passive fraud occurs when _____

    _____

    D. Misrepresentation is _____

    _____

8-3 Mistake

    A. A unilateral mistake does not offer _____

    _____

    B. A bilateral mistake allows _____

    _____

    C. Mutual mistakes that are grounds for rescission are

        1. _____

        2. _____

        3. _____

    D. Misunderstandings of existing laws do not _____

8-4 Duress and Undue Influence

    A. Physical duress involves either _____

    _____

    B. Economic duress consists of _____

    C. Undue influence occurs when _____

    _____

Legal Concepts

For each statement, write T *in the answer column if the statement is true or* F *if the statement is false.*

Answer

1. Mutual assent evolves through the communication of an offer and an acceptance between the contracting parties.

   1. _____

2. Fraud may arise either from a party's intentional false statement or from the concealment of material facts and conditions.

   2. *T* _____

3. The turning back of a car's odometer may be considered to be a perpetration of active fraud.

   3. *F* _____

4. The term *misrepresentation* is synonymous with fraud.

   4. *F* _____

5. Exaggerated arguments and opinions made by salespersons to induce customers to buy their products are considered to be perpetrations of fraud.

   5. _____

6. Passive conduct that is intended to deceive is fraudulent.

   6. _____

7. In both fraud and misrepresentation the injured party is permitted to terminate the contract and sue for damages.

   7. _____

8. A mistake of a material fact, when made by both contracting parties, is grounds for contract rescission.

   8. *T* _____

9. A unilateral mistake made by an innocent purchaser of goods gives that purchaser the right to return the goods and demand the return of any money already paid for them.

   9. *F* _____

10. Proof that the subject matter of an agreement had been destroyed before the agreement was made is grounds for rescission.

    10. *F* _____

11. Failure to read a document of agreement excuses performance of that agreement.

    11. *F* _____

12. Force or the threat of force, when used in the creation of contractual obligations, is grounds for repudiation of a contract.

    12. _____

13. Economic duress involves a threat to a person's employment or financial security that entices that person to agree to contract obligations.

    13. _____

14. Exposure to public ridicule might constitute economic duress.

    14. _____

15. To prove undue influence, a confidential relationship must be shown to have existed between the parties prior to the agreement in question.

    15. *T* _____

Language of the Law

Select the legal term that best matches each definition.

a. active fraud
b. bilateral mistake
c. concealment
d. confidential relationship
e. duress

f. economic duress
g. emotional duress
h. fiduciary relationship
i. misrepresentation
j. passive fraud

k. physical duress
l. rescission
m. sales puffery
n. undue influence
o. unilateral mistake

Answer

1. Actions or statements made by one contracting party intending to deceive the other contracting party

   1. _____

2. Excessive pressure used by the dominant party in a confidential relationship to convince the weaker party to enter into a contract benefiting the dominant party

   2. _____

3. Threats of exposure to public ridicule

   3. _____

4. An association based upon trust

   4. _____

5. The deliberate nondisclosure or intentional disguise of material facts or conditions that, if known by a contracting party, would significantly affect that party's contractual decision

   5. *C* _____

6. Innocently making a false statement without the intent to deceive

   6. *I* _____

7. A mistake made by both contracting parties 7. _B____

8. Inducing a party to assent to a contract through the use or threat of violence 8. _____

9. Expressions considered to be persuasive but not allowing rescission on grounds of fraud or misrepresentation 9. _O____

10. A mistake involving only one of the contracting parties 10. _O____

Applying the Law

1. Voke agreed to sell his boat to Poindexter for $450. Unknown to either of them at the time of agreement, the boat had broken apart in a storm the previous night. Why could the agreement be rescinded?

_____

_____

_____

2. Marshall failed to read a contract before signing it. The small print in the written contract contained many terms that were disadvantageous to Marshall. Marshall later claimed that he was not bound to the terms of the contract because he was mistaken about them. Why was

_____

_____

_____

3. Cook entered into a written contract to sell his house to Lynch. Cook knew that an underground drainpipe near the house was broken and caused the cellar to flood during the rainy season. Cook did not tell Lynch about the broken drainpipe, but Lynch discovered it after buying the house and living in it during the next rainy season. Why could Lynch recover money damages from Cook?

_____

_____

_____

4. Brandt offered to sell a table to Porat for $400 but said nothing about the kind of wood it was made of. Porat mistakenly thought that the table was made of solid mahogany and paid the $400 under that assumption. Later, when showing the table to some friends, Porat learned that it was made of pine. Why couldn't Porat rescind the transaction?

_____

_____

_____

5. Meecham signed a written contract to sell her house to Haley for $112,400. Unknown to either of them at the time of agreement, the house had been destroyed by fire earlier that day. For what legal reason could Haley rescind the contract for the sale of the house?

_____

_____

_____

_____

6. Chandler entered into a contract to buy a lot of land from Boland, who knew that Chandler planned to build a factory on it. Later, Chandler learned that the zoning laws of the community would not allow a factory to be built on the property. Why couldn't Chandler rescind the contract to buy the lot from Boland?

_____

_____

_____

7. Capriotti described a car that was being sold to Glenn as the best car ever built by General Motors, one that would pass any other car on the road when it was tuned up. Capriotti also maintained that Glenn could never equal its price in the used car market. Investigation proved all of Capriotti's statements to be false. Why couldn't Glenn recover damages on grounds of fraud?

_____

_____

_____

8. Jamison signed a contract to sell her home based on the buyer's threat that failure to agree to sell would result in Jamison losing her position as credit manager with a firm where the buyer had close connections. Jamison later moved to have the agreement rescinded on grounds of duress. Why would Jamison succeed in repudiating the agreement?

_____

_____

_____

9. Community Hardware Store sold Hawkins a ripsaw that they told him was a crosscut saw. Hawkins did not discover the mistake until he started using the saw two days later. Community Hardware refused to refund Hawkins's money or make an exchange. Why could Hawkins return the saw and recover the money paid?

_____

_____

_____

10. Calvarese examined a car being sold by Milltown Motors. She observed that the tires had little remaining tread, that the car showed signs of accident-related damage, and that the car had been recently repainted to conceal the damage. The salesperson stated that the car had always received excellent care, had good tires, had the original paint, and had never been in an accident. Calvarese bought the car and later attempted to rescind the agreement on grounds of fraud. Why would she be unsuccessful in this attempt?

_____

_____

_____

9 Contractual Capacity

Chapter Outline

9-1 Minors' Rights and Obligations

A. When minors disaffirm contracts they are entitled to _____ _____

B. A person becomes an adult _____ _____

C. When minors lie about their age, most states _____ _____

9-2 Contractual Capacity of Minors

A. A minor's contract for necessaries is _____ _____

    1. Necessaries are _____ _____

    2. In determining whether goods and services are necessaries, the court will _____ _____ _____

B. Minors may not disaffirm

    1. _____

    2. _____

C. People may ratify their contracts made during minority only after _____ _____

D. A minor may disaffirm an agreement _____ _____

9-3 Persons with Mental Impairments and Persons Drugged or Intoxicated

A. A contract made by someone who is mentally ill may be valid if _____ _____ _____

B. Persons declared by a court to be insane are _____ _____ _____

C. A contract agreed to by someone under the influence of alcohol or drugs is _____ _____ _____ _____

Legal Concepts

For each statement, write T *in the answer column if the statement is true or* F *if the statement is false.*

Answer

1. The presumption that anyone entering into a contractual relationship has the legal capacity to do so is rebuttable.

    1. _____

2. A person reaches legal age on the anniversary of his or her birth.

    2. _____

3. In most states, if a minor disaffirms a contract, the minor is entitled to a return of everything paid to the other party of the contract.

    3. *T*

4. Necessaries, as related to minors' contracts, vary with the financial and social status of each particular minor.

    4. _____

5. In all states, minors who are married may not disaffirm their contracts.

    5. _____

6. Continuing to accept the benefits of a contract after having reached majority affirms or ratifies an otherwise voidable contract.

    6. _____

7. In most cases, parents are not liable for contracts executed by their minor children unless the parents have co-signed a contract.

    7. _____

8. Minors may, at their option, disaffirm a valid marriage.

    8. _____

9. After reaching legal age, adults may not disaffirm an agreement made during minority.

    9. _____

10. A person who has a voidable title to personal property may transfer a valid title to an innocent purchaser of that property.

    10. _____

11. All agreements made by mental incompetents are void.

    11. _____

12. A minor who has sold real estate to someone who later sells it to an innocent third party may, on reaching adulthood, disaffirm and recover the real property.

    12. _____

13. Persons declared to be legally insane are denied the right to enter into contracts.

    13. _____

14. Minors may, at their option, disaffirm a valid contract for enlistment in the armed forces.

    14. _____

15. A contract agreed to by a person under the influence of alcohol may be voidable if the intoxicated party has lost the ability to comprehend the obligations under the contract.

    15. *T*

Language of the Law

Select the legal term that best matches each definition.

a. abandoned
b. affirmance
c. age of majority
d. capacity
e. disaffirm

f. emancipated
g. executory
h. incompetents
i. intoxication
j. luxuries

k. minor
l. necessaries
m. ratification
n. rebuttable presumption
o. voidable

Answer

1. Freed from observing the laws regulating rights and obligations of minors' contracts

    1. *F*

2. Title received by anyone buying something from a minor

    2. *O*

3. Goods and services that are essential to a minor's health and welfare

    3. *L*

4. To show by a statement or act the intent not to live up to a voidable contract

    4. *E*

5. The day before a person's birthday

    5. _____

6. The legal ability to enter into a contractual relationship

    6. _____

7. Parties deemed to be incapable of entering into enforceable agreements

    7. _____

8. Not fully performed by both parties

    8. _____

9. A promise or act made by a person reaching the age of majority that makes an agreement made during minority valid rather than voidable (select two answers)

    9. _____

10. A person who has not yet reached the age of majority

    10. _____

Applying the Law

1. On her seventeenth birthday, Parsons withdrew $1,000 from her savings account and bought a camcorder outfit from a local store. After using the camcorder for six months, Parsons returned the camcorder to the store and asked for her money back. Why was the store required to return the money Parsons paid for the camcorder?

_____

_____

2. Sousa, a minor, purchased a secondhand car from Andrews for $850. Three months later, Sousa accidentally ran into a tree, and the car was totaled. Sousa had the wreck towed to Andrews's house and demanded the return of the $850. For what legal reason would Sousa's demand be upheld by the court?

_____

_____

3. Perez bought a boat from Ingalls on the day before Perez's eighteenth birthday. A week later he took the boat back to Ingalls, said that he was disaffirming the contract on the ground of minority, and asked for his money back. Ingalls refused Perez's request, and Perez brought suit. Why would the court hold in favor of Ingalls?

_____

_____

4. Glancy agreed to make ten payments of $40 each for a stereo he bought from Rodriguez. On his eighteenth birthday, Glancy made the first installment payment. The next day, Glancy returned the stereo and demanded the return of his money on the grounds that he was a minor when he entered the contract. Why doesn't Rodriguez have to honor Glancy's request?

_____

_____

5. Leeds was declared insane by a court and had a guardian appointed to handle her affairs. She wandered away from home one day, went to a nearby mall, and purchased $4,000 worth of jewelry with her credit card, which had never been canceled. She then walked to the beach and threw the jewelry into the ocean. Why would neither Leeds nor her guardian have to pay the $4,000 that is owed to the jewelry store?

_____

_____

6. Adams, 17 years old, signed a contract for a new car. Included in the contract was this statement: "I attest to the fact that at the time of signing this agreement I have reached age eighteen." Adams paid a small down payment and used the car for long trips during the following month. He now proposes to disaffirm the agreement. Why would Adams be permitted to avoid the contract and have no further responsibility to the seller?

_____

_____

_____

7. Burell, a minor, sold certain property to Noyes at a reasonable price. Two years after reaching his majority, Burell demanded the return of his property and offered to return the money received for it. Noyes refused. Why couldn't Burell recover the property sold to Noyes?

_____

_____

_____

8. Shockley, a wealthy 16-year-old orphan, ordered his tailor to make him a warm winter coat at a cost of $225. When his coat was ready, Shockley informed the tailor that he had changed his mind and was voiding their agreement. Why could the tailor force Shockley to pay for the coat, even though Shockley had not yet reached his majority?

_____

_____

_____

9. Turner agreed while intoxicated to sell his diamond ring, worth $350, to Murton for $50. The next day Turner changed his mind and refused to carry out the agreement. Murton brought suit against Turner for damages. Why would Murton be unsuccessful in this suit?

_____

_____

_____

10. Rubin was known to neighbors and friends as being mentally incompetent. The state had never declared her insane because no one had ever been endangered by her actions. Teen Shop agreed to sell Rubin a coat. The shop did not recognize her lack of reasoning powers. The coat was a necessary. Why could Rubin be held liable for the cost of the coat?

_____

_____

_____

10 Consideration

Chapter Outline

10-1 Requirements of Consideration

A. Consideration consists of _____
_____

B. A detriment is any of the following
1. _____
2. _____
3. _____

C. An agreement involves a bargained-for exchange when
1. _____
2. _____
3. _____

10-2 Types of Consideration

A. Money is _____
_____

B. The courts have held that barter agreements contain _____
_____

C. Promising not to sue is called _____

D. When pledges are made to fund a specific project, the pledgee's sacrifice is _____

10-3 Problems with Consideration

A. If a creditor accepts as full payment an amount that is disputed, then _____
_____

B. A part payment in lieu of full payment will not cancel _____
_____

10-4 Agreements Without Consideration

A. In some states, a seal takes the place of _____
_____

B. Persons discharged from indebtedness through bankruptcy may _____
_____

C. Debtors may revive and reaffirm debts barred by the statutes of limitations without
_____
_____

D. Promissory estoppel is _____
_____

E. The Uniform Commercial Code (UCC) has made an exception to the rule requiring
_____

F. Illusory promises fail to provide _____

G. A promise of a gift is _____

_____

H. Past consideration is not _____

I. A promise to do something that is already obligated to do cannot be _____

_____

Legal Concepts

For each statement, write T *in the answer column if the statement is true or* F *if the statement is false.*

Answer

1. Consideration consists of a mutual exchange of benefits and sacrifices between contracting parties.

1. T

2. The law will not enforce an agreement that has not been bargained for.

2. _____

3. Refraining from doing that which one has a legal right to do is valid consideration.

3. _____

4. The benefits and detriments exchanged as consideration must be legal.

4. _____

5. The concept of bargaining means that one person gains something and the other person loses something.

5. _____

6. The courts have held that barter agreements contain no valid consideration.

6. _____

7. When the right to sue exists, a promise not to sue is enforceable when supported by consideration.

7. T

8. A pledge of money to a charitable institution is unenforceable because the charity gives no consideration.

8. _____

9. The courts will entertain arguments based on accord and satisfaction even in trivial and superficial disputes.

9. _____

10. When accepted by a creditor, a partial payment in lieu of full payment will cancel an undisputed debt.

10. _____

11. In some states, a seal gives a written contract the presumption of consideration.

11. _____

12. Debtors may revive and reaffirm debts barred by the statutes of limitations without the necessity of new consideration.

12. _____

13. A promise to give someone a gift at some future time is enforceable with no consideration.

13. _____

14. Past consideration makes an agreement binding.

14. _____

15. A promise to carry out an act that one is already obligated to do by law or contract is valid consideration to support a contract.

15. F

Language of the Law

Select the legal term that best matches each definition.

a. accord
b. accord and satisfaction
c. bargained-for exchange
d. consideration
e. detriment

f. disputed amount
g. estoppel
h. forbearance
i. option
j. past consideration

k. preexisting duty
l. release
m. statutes of limitations
n. unconscionable
o. undisputed amount

Answer

1. Refraining from doing something that one has a legal right to do

1. _____

2. A court's opinion that a ridiculously inadequate amount of consideration is involved in a contract

2. _____

3. The giving of consideration to support an offeror's promise to hold an offer open for a reasonable length of time

3. I

4. Statutes that specify the time period within which action on a contract must begin
5. Doing something that one has a legal right to do
6. The implied or expressed acceptance by a creditor of less than the amount owed by a debtor
7. A promise to do something that one is already obligated to do by law or by some other promise or agreement
8. A doctrine that denies to a complaining party rights that are shown to be the cause of that party's own injury
9. A promise of consideration made to a party after that party has already performed an act for the benefit of the promisor
10. The exchange of benefits and sacrifices by contracting parties that creates a binding agreement

4. _____
5. _E_____
6. _____
7. _____
8. _____
9. _____
10. _D_____

Applying the Law

1. Osgood agreed to sell a cassette deck "boom box" to King for $75; King agreed to buy it for that price. Later, King tried to rescind the transaction. King claimed that there was no consideration in the agreement because he had not yet paid the $75 and Osgood had not yet given him the cassette deck. Why is King incorrect?

_____

_____

2. Matta agreed to sell a large quantity of cocaine to Davis for $2 million and Davis agreed to buy it for that price. Davis failed to carry out his part of the deal. Why does this agreement have no consideration?

_____

_____

3. Schultz drove his motor vehicle through a red light and smashed into a car driven by Chandler. Chandler had an estimate made of the damage to his vehicle and agreed to forget the matter if Schultz would pay him $465. Schultz agreed to pay the money if Chandler would sign a written promise not to sue. Why would such a promise contain consideration and be binding on Chandler?

_____

_____

4. Debronsky promised her brother that she would leave him $50,000 in her will. On Debronsky's death, her brother discovered that his sister left him only $100. He sued to enforce the promise his sister had made before her death. Why would the brother be unsuccessful in this action?

_____

_____

5. O'Neill, a police officer, agreed to pay special attention to Arnold's home while Arnold was on vacation. Arnold's property was on O'Neill's regular beat, and Arnold agreed to pay O'Neill $50 for the protection given. If Arnold failed to pay the $50, why would O'Neill be unable to collect the promised payment through court action?

_____

_____

_____

6. Hancock Furniture Company promised, in a written contract, to purchase any cherry wood "as it may desire" from Forestry Products Corporation. Hancock then purchased cherry wood from another source at a much better price. Why would Forestry Products Corporation have no legal recourse against Hancock?

_____

_____

7. Zigmont purchased 100 gallons of gasoline from Oakwood Service Station at a rate of one dollar per gallon. Zigmont later learned that all other service stations in the city charged only 90 cents per gallon. Zigmont sent a check to Oakwood for $90 with the notation "In full payment for the 100 gallons of gasoline purchased from your station." Oakwood deposited the check. Why could Oakwood still demand the ten-dollar balance on Zigmont's bill?

_____

_____

8. Dr. Saltzer performed an operation on Hartmann. Hartmann received a bill for $1,500 instead of for the $500 the surgeon had led him to expect. He was angered and sent Saltzer a check for $500, writing on the back "In full payment for all professional services." The doctor cashed the check, indorsing it below Hartmann's notation. Why did the doctor have no recourse against Hartmann for the balance of $1,000?

_____

_____

9. Sanders assisted two elderly women whose car was stranded in a snowbank during a blizzard. More than an hour was required to get the car back on the highway. "Young man, we appreciate your great kindness," the women said. "We promise that we will mail you a check for $25 for your work and time." Why couldn't Sanders enforce this promise if the check is not sent?

_____

_____

10. Dukes pledged $400 to a church that was planning to install a new organ. When the work was finished, she refused to honor the pledge. Dukes argued that since she had received no benefit, there was no consideration to support her pledge. Why could she be sued for the $400?

_____

_____

11 Legality

Chapter Outline

11-1 Agreements to Engage in Unlawful Activity

A. The law cannot honor an agreement for which the objective is _____ _____ _____

B. The law will not uphold any contract that involves a promise to _____ _____ _____

11-2 Agreements Made Illegal Under Statutory Law

Some activities that are illegal by statute are

A. _____

B. _____

C. _____

D. _____

E. _____

11-3 Agreements Contrary to Public Policy

Some agreements that are void because they are against public policy are

A. _____

B. _____

C. _____

D. _____

E. _____

11-4 Consequences of Illegality

A. When an entire agreement is tainted with illegality, _____ _____ _____

B. When a divisible agreement is tainted with illegality, _____ _____ _____ _____

Legal Concepts

For each statement, write T *in the answer column if the statement is true or* F *if the statement is false.*

Answer

1. The law will not honor an agreement to commit a crime.   1. _____
2. An agreement to commit a tort would be valid in the eyes of the law.   2. _____
3. Wagering agreements are not affected by statutory law.   3. _____

4. Businesses and professions are licensed solely as a means of collecting additional taxes for public use.

5. Contracts entered into on Sunday are invalid in all 50 states.

6. The enforcement of "blue laws" varies widely from state to state, county to county, and village to village.

7. Agreements made with the intent of suppressing competition or fixing prices are illegal restraints of trade and therefore void.

8. Any action that tends to harm the health, safety, welfare, or morals of the public is said to violate public policy.

9. An agreement to give false testimony at a trial is enforceable.

10. An agreement that tends to interfere with the service and proper performance of a public official is void as contrary to public policy.

11. Agreements that tend to weaken the rights of creditors are void.

12. The law looks with disfavor on agreements that allow parties to escape liability for their own wrongdoing.

13. Restrictive employment covenants must be reasonable in the type of work prohibited, the length of time involved, and the geographical area covered.

14. The rule of *in pari delicto* applies to agreements in which both parties are equally wrong and equally at fault.

15. Exculpatory clauses, when part of an otherwise valid and legal agreement, ordinarily are enforceable as a matter of public policy.

4. _____
5. _____
6. _____
7. _____
8. _____
9. _____
10. _____
11. _____
12. _____
13. _I_____
14. _____
15. _____

Language of the Law

Select the legal term that best matches each definition.

a. blue laws
b. conspiracy
c. divisible
d. exculpatory agreement
e. *in pari delicto*

f. indivisible
g. licensing
h. local option
i. obstruction of justice
j. public policy

k. restraint of trade
l. restrictive covenant
m. unconscionable
n. usury
o. wager

Answer

1. Able to be separated into two parts
2. A procedure that allows regulation and supervision of business and professions
3. A limitation on the full exercise of doing business with others
4. A clause in an agreement to sell a business that restricts the seller from entering the same type of business
5. So grossly unfair as to shock the court's conscience
6. In equal fault
7. A device used in the attempt to escape legal responsibility
8. State laws that either limit or prohibit commercial transactions and certain other activities on Sunday
9. The general legal principle that says no one should be allowed to do anything that injures the public at large
10. Interest charged in excess of the rate permitted by state law

1. _____
2. _____
3. _K_____
4. _____
5. _____
6. _____
7. _____
8. _____
9. _J_____
10. _____

Applying the Law

1. Leach's video rental shop was not doing well because another video shop in the same community rented tapes at a cheaper rate. Leach offered to pay Brazelton $2,000 if Brazelton would break into the competitor's shop and destroy the competitor's tapes. Brazelton agreed to do so but failed to carry out the transaction. Why was the agreement void?

_____

_____

2. Neumann borrowed $1,000 from Reymo and agreed to pay Reymo $25 per day in interest until the loan was paid back. Why was the loan agreement illegal and void?

_____

_____

3. Bard entered into a contract with Kirshner to buy fishing equipment for $75, a boat for $300, and a machine gun for $500. Machine gun sales were illegal in that state. Bard later breached the contract. Why will the court enforce all of the contract except the part concerning the machine gun?

_____

_____

4. Metcalf, a 91-year-old widow, signed a contract to have vinyl siding placed on her bungalow for $150,000. On what grounds could Metcalf void the contract?

_____

_____

5. Dugan was an Air Force pilot but had never received a civilian pilot's license. Raskob hired him to fly a twin-engine aircraft from Denver to Detroit for $250 and expenses. Why couldn't Dugan collect the money owed if Raskob refused payment when Dugan landed in Detroit?

_____

_____

6. Langes sold a restaurant to Govatos for $25,000. As part of the agreement, Langes promised not to open another restaurant business for ten years within a 50-mile radius of the one sold. Why was this agreement unenforceable against Langes?

_____

_____

7. Roberts specialized in chemical research for Hughes Chemical Company. Roberts had access to all secret materials that had resulted from research in this area by the company over a ten-year period. In her employment contract, Roberts had agreed not to accept employment with a competing firm for five years after the Hughes contract expired. Why was this employment contract not an illegal restraint of trade?

_____

_____

_____

8. Fairton witnessed an accident at the corner of Broad and Chestnut streets. One of the drivers offered him $200 cash if he would disappear and not claim to be a witness. He accepted the $200. Three days later, Fairton offered testimony to the police department about what had happened. Why could Fairton not be sued for breach of the agreement with the driver?

_____

_____

_____

9. Hines and O'Neal operated separate radio and television repair shops in Center County. These shops were the only ones offering repair service. Hines and O'Neal agreed on new and higher rates that each would charge for work done. Why would this agreement be unenforceable if O'Neal were to offer old rates and advertise for additional customers on the basis of the lower prices?

_____

_____

_____

10. Gutierrez, a city building inspector and engineer, agreed to approve improper concrete work that had been done on the Hightower Building. Owners of the building promised to appoint Gutierrez to the position of building manager in return for the favors extended by the inspector. The Hightower Building's owners failed to carry out their agreement with Gutierrez. Why couldn't she recover damages through their breach of this agreement?

_____

_____

_____

12 Form of the Agreement

Chapter Outline

12-1 The Statute of Frauds

A. Contracts that must be in writing to be enforceable are

1. _____
2. _____
3. _____
4. _____
5. _____
6. _____

B. A written memorandum should contain the following elements:

1. _____
2. _____
3. _____
4. _____
5. _____

12-2 Special Rules Involving Written Contracts

A. The parol evidence rule says _____
_____
_____

B. Under the best evidence rule, courts will accept only _____
_____
_____

C. The parol evidence rule does not apply to

1. _____
2. _____
3. _____
4. _____
5. _____

D. The equal dignities rule provides that _____
_____
_____

12-3 Formalities of Contract Construction

A. The legal signature of a person is _____
_____

B. In most documents, witnesses are _____
_____

C. Today's seal is usually nothing more than _____
_____

D. Certain documents may be recorded in a public office for inspection by _____
_____

Legal Concepts

For each statement, write T *in the answer column if the statement is true of* F *if the statement is false.*

Answer

1. Most contracts must be in writing to be enforceable.
1. ___F___
2. If the terms of a contract make it impossible to complete the contract within one year, the contract must be in writing.
2. ___F___
3. Contracts for the sale of land valued at less than $500 may be either oral or written.
3. ___F___
4. Contracts for the transfer or sale of any interest in land do not necessarily have to be in writing.
4. _____
5. A lease for the renting of another's real property must be in writing unless it is for a period of less than one year.
5. _____
6. Contracts for the sale of goods must be in writing when the property price is $500 or less.
6. ___F___
7. Under international law (CISG), contracts for the sale of goods need not be in writing.
7. _____
8. A promise to answer for and pay someone else's debts must be in writing to be enforceable.
8. _____
9. Agreements in consideration of marriage must be in writing, but the marriage contract itself need not be.
9. _____
10. To satisfy the Statute of Frauds, a memorandum need not identify both parties to be obligated under the contract.
10. _____
11. On a memorandum, the only signature needed to satisfy the Statute of Frauds is that of the party sought to be bound to the agreement.
11. _____
12. Evidence of oral statements made before the signing of a written agreement is usually admissible in court to change the terms of the written agreement.
12. _____
13. The courts, under the best evidence rule, will accept only the original of a writing and not a copy.
13. _____
14. A signature may be a person's full name or initials and may be printed, typewritten, or stamped (as with a rubber stamp).
14. _____
15. The equal dignities rule provides that when someone appoints an agent to negotiate an agreement that must be in writing, the appointment of the agent may be oral.
15. _____

Language of the Law

Select the legal term that best matches each definition.

a. administrator
b. best evidence rule
c. equal dignities rule
d. executor
e. general release

f. guaranty of payment
g. *locus sigilli*
h. memorandum
i. notary public
j. parol evidence rule

k. prenuptial agreement
l. recorded
m. seal
n. signature
o. Statute of Frauds

Answer

1. An agreement in which two people planning to marry agree to change the property rights that usually arise in marriage
1. _____
2. Evidence of oral statements made before signing a written agreement is usually not admissible in court to contradict or change the terms of the written agreement
2. _____
3. Courts accept as evidence only the original of a writing
3. _____

46

4. When an agent is appointed to negotiate an agreement that must be in writing, the appointment of the agent must also be in writing

4. _____

5. A person appointed to carry out the provisions of a will when an executor is not named or for some reason fails to serve

5. _____

6. British law, now incorporated in state statutes, specifying the agreements that must be in writing if they are to be enforceable as law

6. _O_____

7. Place of the seal

7. _____

8. A person who has legal authority to certify a signature to a document

8. _____

9. Placed in an office for inspection by the public

9. _____

10. Any mark that the maker intends to be a signature

10. _____

Applying the Law

1. A week before they were married, Jacobs and Trammell agreed orally that if their marriage did not last, Jacobs would receive the real estate they owned and Trammell would receive the remainder of their property. Would this agreement be upheld by the court? Explain.

_____

_____

_____

2. Hernandez orally agreed to sell her computer printer to Heath for $350. She later tried to back out of the deal on the grounds that the oral agreement was unenforceable. Would a court hold Hernandez to her promise? Why or why not?

_____

_____

_____

3. In a lawsuit against Feingold, Penders attempted to introduce into evidence a photocopy of a contract the parties had signed. Was the copy allowed into evidence by the court? Explain.

_____

_____

_____

4. Gretto was named administrator of Hall's estate. In defense of Hall's widow, who was threatened with suit unless certain bills of Hall's were paid immediately, Gretto said, "Leave my sister-in-law be. You'll get your money. If things get worse, I'll pay the bills myself." In consideration of this promise, the creditors withdrew their threats. If the accounts are not settled by the estate, could Gretto be charged for the creditors' losses? Why or why not?

_____

_____

_____

5. Zelinski entered into an oral agreement appointing Farm Realty Company as his agent to sign a contract to sell Zelinski's 125-acre farm and buildings for $225,000. Farm Realty signed a contract with a buyer who gave a down payment. Zelinski personally secured another buyer who agreed to pay $250,000 for the property. Was Zelinski obligated to the contract made for him by Farm Realty Company? Explain.

_____

_____

_____

6. Dolan was interviewed for a job on Thursday. The interview was successful, and she agreed orally to start working the following Monday, to be employed from that day, Monday, for one year thereafter. Three weeks after starting the job Dolan was fired without cause and replaced by the employer's niece. Would Dolan be successful in an action brought against the employer for damages? Explain.

_____

_____

_____

7. Angus, a former professional football player, suffered from a crippling disease and lost the use of his right arm. He was offered the job of television announcer for the season of games in his former league. The contract required Angus's signature, which he was not able to affix to the contract. What other procedures could be taken to ensure that Angus's signature would be affixed to the contract?

_____

_____

_____

8. Archino wrote to Katz, offering to sell a diamond ring to Katz for $7,800. Katz replied by return mail, accepting the offer. Archino discovered that the ring would bring more money at an auction and sought to cancel the agreement, arguing that the Statute of Frauds required personal property sales above $500 to be in writing. Could Katz enforce the agreement? Why or why not?

_____

_____

_____

9. LeBlanc purchased four tires from Central Tire Company. Aparicio, her boyfriend, telephoned Central Tire to promise that if LeBlanc failed to honor her bill, he would pay it himself. On this basis, Central Tire proceeded to mount the tires on LeBlanc's car. She did not honor her bill. Could Aparicio be held liable on his telephoned promise to pay LeBlanc's bill? Explain.

_____

_____

_____

10. Jeness signed a contract agreeing to purchase a used car for $2,080. The sales representative of Guarantee Motors explained that the car would be guaranteed for six months for all labor and parts that might be needed to make necessary repairs. The written contract contained nothing about the warranty. Jeness had severe and expensive difficulties with the car and returned the vehicle to Guarantee Motors for the repairs promised under the agreement with the firm's representative. Would Jeness's demands for performance of the guarantee be upheld? Why or why not?

_____

_____

_____

13 Third Parties in Contract Law

Chapter Outline

13-1 Third Parties and Operation of Contracts

A. The most frequently recognized intended beneficiaries are

1. _____

2. _____

3. _____

B. An incidental beneficiary is _____

_____

13-2 Assignment of Contracts

A. Rights are assigned and duties are _____

B. The parties to an assignment are

1. _____

2. _____

3. _____

C. To create an assignment, consideration is _____

_____

_____

D. Assignments may be accomplished through _____

_____

_____

E. An assignee should give notice of the assignment to _____

_____

F. The rights and duties of an assignee are _____

_____

_____

G. A party may not delegate duties that _____

_____

H. Parties to a contract may include a condition that will _____

_____

I. Assignments, in special situations, may be restricted by _____

_____

13-3 Novation

A. If all three parties agree, the assignor can be _____

_____

B. A novation is _____

_____

Legal Concepts

For each statement, write T *in the answer column if the statement is true or* F *if the statement is false.*

1. Third parties are at times given benefits from a contract made between two other parties.
2. Donee beneficiaries have no legal grounds to bring suit for acts promised by contracting parties.
3. Incidental beneficiaries have legal grounds for enforcing the contract made by those in privity of contract.
4. Consideration is not required in the creation of an assignment.
5. Assignments may be accomplished through written, oral, or implied agreements between the assignor and the assignee.
6. The law permits the assignment of all types of valid and enforceable executory contracts.
7. In an assignment, "the assignee steps into the shoes of the assignor."
8. The assignor is obligated to any express and implied warranties that serve to protect either the assignee or the obligor.
9. There is an implied warranty that duties owed to an obligor will be carried out in a complete and satisfactory manner by an assignee.
10. One may usually delegate duties that are of a personal or professional service nature.
11. Rights are generally delegated and duties are generally assigned.
12. The right of assignment may be restricted by agreement of the parties.
13. Members of the armed forces may assign their pay to whomever they wish.
14. The assignor, rather than the assignee, is required to notify the obligor of an assignment.
15. Novations differ from assignments in that a novation is an entirely new agreement.

1. _T_____
2. _____
3. _F_____
4. _____
5. _____
6. _F_____
7. _T_____
8. _____
9. _____
10. _____
11. _____
12. _____
13. _____
14. _____
15. _____

Language of the Law

Select the legal term that best matches each definition.

a. assignee
b. assignment
c. assignor
d. beneficiary
e. creditor beneficiary
f. delegation
g. donee beneficiary
h. incidental beneficiary
i. insurance beneficiary
j. intended beneficiary
k. novation
l. obligor
m. outside party
n. third party
o. warranty

1. One who is named to receive the benefits guaranteed under an insurance policy
2. A third party who does not provide any consideration for benefits received and who does not owe the contracting parties any legal duties
3. A transfer of a contract right
4. The remaining party to the original agreement after an assignment takes place
5. A transfer of a contract duty
6. Someone who could benefit indirectly from a contract performance but whose benefit was not of concern when the contract was made; this person cannot sue to recover any benefits
7. One who transfers contract rights to another
8. A third party who receives benefits from a contract made by others
9. The creation of a new contract to replace one in which the performance has not yet commenced or has been only partly executed
10. A promise, statement, or other representation that an item has certain qualities

1. _____
2. _____
3. _____
4. _____
5. _____
6. __h_____
7. _____
8. _____
9. _____
10. _____

Applying the Law

1. Davis owed Prue $250. Prue told Davis to give the money to Prue's nephew, Weeks, as a college graduation present from Prue. Before the money was paid, however, Prue canceled the assignment and told Davis to pay Prue the money instead. Would Weeks have a cause of action against Prue? Explain.

_____

_____

_____

2. Adams was owed $20,000 by Hull. In payment for a yacht, Adams assigned the right to receive the $20,000 to Christo. Christo did not notify Hull of the assignment, and Hull paid the $20,000 to Adams. Adams went bankrupt. Would Christo lose the $20,000? Why or why not?

_____

_____

_____

3. Gross entered into a contract to sell 1,000 cases of computer paper to Morris for $5,000. Later, Gross delegated to Zito the task of selling the paper to Morris. Gross also assigned to Zito the right to receive the $5,000. Morris did not agree to either the delegation or the assignment. Gross claimed that this was a novation. Was Gross correct? Explain.

_____

_____

_____

4. Dr. Gravers, an obstetrician, accepted O'Leary as a patient during the period of her pregnancy and delivery. Eight months later, Gravers informed O'Leary that he planned to take a vacation in Bermuda. Without O'Leary's permission, Gravers assigned the case to Dr. Harrison, an equally reputable and skillful obstetrician. O'Leary claimed that she didn't have to go to the new doctor. Was O'Leary correct?

_____

_____

_____

5. Langley paid premiums on a contract of fire insurance in which Rawlins, a partner, was named as beneficiary in event of a fire loss. The insurer agreed to these terms, but when a fire loss arose, the company refused to pay the amount of the proved loss to the named beneficiary, claiming that the beneficiary had not given any consideration in return for this unearned benefit. Was the insurance company liable to Langley's named beneficiary? Why or why not?

_____

_____

_____

6. The Gulf Bridge Authority contracted with Salakas Painting Contractors for the repainting of all steelwork on the bridge. It was agreed that Salakas would use Continental Paint, a particular brand, on the job. It was later discovered that paint manufactured by another firm had been used in painting the bridge. Could Continental Paint Company recover damages from Salakas for failure to use its paint as provided in the contract with Gulf Bridge Authority? Why or why not?

_____

_____

_____

7. Jenkins entered into a written contract to buy a parcel of real estate from Harcourt for $125,000. Before the contract was carried out, Jenkins assigned his rights un- der the contract to Campbell through a telephone conversation. Was the assignment enforceable? Why or why not?

_____

_____

_____

8. In the above case, would the assignment to Campbell have been enforceable had the written contract between Jenkins and Harcourt stated, "Neither party may assign this contract without the express permission of the other party thereto"? Why or why not?

_____

_____

_____

9. Howell agreed to paint Ortega's house for $2,000 provided that Ortega would pay the money to Howell's daughter. If Howell painted the house and Ortega failed to pay the $2,000, would Howell's daughter have the right to bring suit? Why or why not?

_____

_____

_____

10. Carter hired Wintersteen, a well-known artist, to paint her portrait. Due to an overload of work, Wintersteen delegated the task of painting Carter's portrait to Regan, a budding art student. Was Carter bound to the delegation? Why or why not?

_____

_____

_____

14 Discharge and Remedies

Chapter Outline

14-1 Discharge by Performance

A. When time for performance is not stated in the contract, the contract must be performed _____

B. When the time for performance is stated in the contract but nothing indicates that time is of particular importance, _____

_____

C. When the phrase *time is of the essence* is included among the terms of a written contract, _____

D. When there is no express agreement as to satisfaction of performance, the law implies _____

E. Substantial performance results when _____

_____

F. Conditions in contracts may be classified as

1. _____

2. _____

3. _____

G. Tender of performance means _____

_____

14-2 Discharge by Nonperformance

A. When a contract is discharged by agreement

1. Mutual rescission requires _____

_____

2. Termination by waiver occurs when _____

_____

3. Accord and satisfaction means _____

_____

B. When the subject matter of a contract has been destroyed when the contract is entered into, _____

C. Death, insanity, or disability of a party _____

_____

D. Examples of discharge by operation of law are

1. _____

2. _____

E. Breach of contracts comes from

    1. _____

    2. _____

    3. _____

14-3 Remedies

A. A breach of contract releases _____

B. Damages are of different kinds

    1. Actual damages are _____

    2. Incidental damages cover _____

    3. Consequential damages result _____

    4. Punitive damages are _____

    5. Nominal damages are _____

    6. *Quantum meruit* means _____

    7. Liquidated damages are _____

C. The injured party has an obligation to _____

D. Two equitable remedies are

    1. _____

    2. _____

Legal Concepts

For each statement, write T *in the answer column if the statement is true or* F *if the statement is false.*

Answer

1. Most contracts are discharged through performance.   1. _T_____
2. Ordinarily, substantial performance does not discharge a contract.   2. _____
3. Satisfactory performance is not a condition of every contract.   3. _____
4. In a unilateral contract, the performance of a condition precedent serves as the offeree's acceptance of the offer.   4. _____
5. Courts usually enforce time stipulations in a contract even when time is not of particular importance.   5. _____
6. Even though a contract is in writing, an agreed-to rescission is valid if expressed orally.   6. _____
7. It is not important to make tender even if one knows the other party is not going to perform the contract.   7. _____
8. Destruction of specific subject matter applicable to an executory contract discharges the contract.   8. _T_____
9. Most contractual obligations to pay money do not come to an end when a party files for bankruptcy.   9. _F_____
10. When performance of a contract is made illegal by the passage of laws after the formation of the contract, nonperformance is excusable, and the contract may be discharged.   10. _____
11. Death, disability, or insanity will always discharge the incapacitated party, or the party's estate, from performance of contractual promises.   11. _____
12. The statute of limitations sets forth specific time periods during which actions may be taken for the collection of debts, claims of damages through torts, and the prosecution of certain crimes.   12. _T_____
13. The usual remedy for breach of contract is the payment of money.   13. _T_____
14. A court can order specific performance of a contract for the sale of land.   14. _____
15. Courts allow speculative damages in some cases.   15. _____

Language of the Law

Select the legal term that best matches each definition.

a. abandonment of contractual obligations
b. anticipatory breach
c. complete performance
d. condition concurrent
e. condition precedent
f. consequential damages
g. discharge
h. general release
i. incidental damages
j. injunction
k. nominal damages
l. satisfactory performance
m. specific performance
n. substantial performance
o. termination by waiver

Answer

1. Token damages awarded to parties who have experienced an injury to their legal rights but no actual loss
1. _____
2. A condition that occurs when both parties fully accomplish every term, condition, and promise to which they agree
2. _____
3. The performance of a contract according to the agreement
3. _____
4. Stopping performance once it has begun
4. _____
5. A condition that requires both parties to perform at the same time
5. _____
6. An award made when a contract is breached to cover expenses incurred by the innocent party in attempting to prevent further loss
6. _____
7. An order of the court requiring a breaching party to do what that party promised to do under the terms of the contract
7. _M_
8. An order issued by a court directing that a party do something or refrain from doing something
8. _____
9. The condition that occurs when a party executes all promised terms and conditions of a contract with the exception of minor details
9. _N_
10. A written and signed document intended to terminate and discharge the contractual obligations of a party
10. _____

Applying the Law

1. Benson was hired as accompanist for ten concert appearances with Strosky, an operatic tenor. Halfway through the concert tour, Benson suffered arthritic pains in her right hand, making it impossible to complete her contract. Strosky sued the accompanist for breach of contract, demanding damages for her refusal to continue on the tour. Would Strosky be successful in this action? Why or why not?

_____

_____

2. Damico purchased three suits along with other articles of men's wear from Market Mall Men's Shop, using his revolving charge account. Two payments were made over a period of three months after purchase. The balance remained unpaid for a five-year period despite letters, telephone calls, threats of legal action, and Market Mall's giving the account over to a collection agency. Did Damico have a defense against payment of the balance owed if sued by Market Mall Men's Shop? Why or why not?

_____

_____

3. Softknit Industries contracted to sell 100 dozen infant sleepwear sets to Tender Years, a chain store serving young families over a five-state area. Subsequently, the Consumer Product Safety Commission prohibited the manufacture and sale of infant garments from textiles that Softknit had contracted to use in the agreement with Tender Years. Softknit argued that the restrictive regulation could not be applied to contracts made prior to these new rulings. Was Softknit correct? Explain.

_____

_____

4. McCordy signed a contract for purchase of a new car from ABC Sales Company. The seller breached its agreement by not delivering the car. McCordy sought out another car dealer that sold her the same model of car at the same price she had agreed to pay ABC. If McCordy sued the seller for breach of contract and won, what type of damages would be awarded to her?

_____

_____

5. Stevens Machine Company contracted to build and deliver a 150-horsepower steam engine to Valley Generating Company. Delivery of the engine was promised for November 15. On June 25, Stevens notified Valley Generating Company that it was repudiating the contract, giving no justifiable reasons for doing so. Valley Generating Company instituted an action for breach of contract immediately. Stevens argued that no action could be brought until after November 15. Was Stevens correct? Why or why not?

_____

_____

6. Marinelli left a television with Lukens Television Repair Shop for testing and necessary repairs. Lukens made tests, found what was wrong, but never commenced actual repairs. Nothing was done on the set for more than three months. After repeated entreaties and calls demanding that the work be done, Marinelli asked for the return of the set. Lukens refused to give up the set unless Marinelli paid the shop for the time spent on making the tests. Was Lukens correct? Explain.

_____

_____

7. The Travellers, a rock group, contracted to play for the regular Friday evening dances at Lacey's Lounge. On Monday the Travellers' manager called Lacey's Lounge, canceling their engagement. Lacey petitioned a court of equity, seeking a decree of specific performance that would have required the Travellers to play their engagement. Would Lacey's Lounge be successful in this petition? Why or why not?

_____

8. Dr. Morgan agreed to direct a team doing basic research in toxic chemicals for Chemical Research & Development Corporation. The term of employment was five years, and Morgan agreed to accept no employment with other firms doing the same work for two years after expiration of the Chemical Research contract. If Morgan does go with another competing firm, could Chemical Research seek relief from a court of equity? Why or why not?

_____

9. Buzby paid a landscape gardener to mow and trim around the Buzby Building. Buzby found that the gardener had missed a few square feet of lawn in the rear of the property. Could Buzby declare the contract breached on grounds of nonperformance? Explain.

_____

10. Kirby contracted to have a new house built by Westwood Home Builders. Among other things, Westwood Home Builders agreed that the project would be completed by April 15. Unforeseen difficulties delayed the interior decorating, and the new house was not ready until May 1. Kirby declared the contract breached and refused payment. Was Kirby correct? Why or why not?

_____

15 Sales and Leases of Goods

Chapter Outline

15-1 The Uniform Commercial Code

Today the Uniform Commercial Code (UCC) has been adopted by _____
_____

15-2 The Sale and Lease of Goods

A. Article 2 of the UCC, which contains the law of sales, applies _____
_____

B. Goods are defined as _____

C. Many of the features that are found in the UCC that relate to the sale of goods also apply to _____

15-3 The Sales Contract

A. A sale is defined as _____
_____

B. A contract to sell occurs when _____
_____

15-4 Special Rules for Sales Contracts

The following special rules apply to sales contracts:

A. _____

B. _____

C. _____

D. _____

E. _____

F. _____

G. _____

H. _____

I. _____

15-5 Form of Sales Contracts

A. A sales contract must be in writing when _____
_____

B. A lease of goods must be in writing if _____
_____

C. The four exceptions to the general rule are

1. _____

2. _____

3. _____

4. _____

D. The writing that is required to satisfy the UCC must

1. indicate that _____

2. mention the _____

3. be signed by _____

15-6 International Sales

A. The United Nations Convention on Contracts for the International Sale of Goods (CISG) applies to sales between _____

_____

B. The CISG does not apply to

1. _____

2. _____

3. _____

4. _____

5. _____

15-7 Auction Sales

In an auction sale,

A. the offer is made by _____

B. the acceptance is made by _____

15-8 Bulk Transfers

The four requirements that must be followed when a bulk transfer is made are

A. _____

B. _____

C. _____

D. _____

Legal Concepts

For each statement, write T *in the answer column if the statement is true or* F *if the statement is false.*

Answer

1. The UCC has been adopted, either in whole or in part, by every state in the United States.

1. _____

2. The law of sales does not apply to transactions between private parties.

2. _____

3. The unborn young of animals are considered to be goods.

3. _T____

4. Fish in the sea are considered to be future goods.

4. _T____

5. When a contract includes both goods and services, the law of sales always applies.

5. _____

6. A gift is considered a sale.

6. _____

7. Consideration is necessary to modify a contract for the sale of goods.

7. _____

8. An enforceable contract for the sale of goods may come about even though some terms are not completely agreed upon.

8. _____

9. No consideration is necessary when a merchant promises in writing to hold an offer open for the sale of goods.

9. _____

10. A contract to buy "all the oil we need to heat our building" is not allowed under the UCC because the quantity of the goods is not definite.

10. _F____

11. An agreement modifying a contract for the sale of goods needs no consideration to be binding.

11. _____

12. Under the UCC, a contract for the sale of goods for the price of $300 or more must be in writing to be enforceable.

12. _____

13. If the seller has made a substantial beginning in manufacturing specially made goods, an oral agreement in any amount is enforceable.

13. _____

14. In an auction without reserve, the auctioneer may withdraw the goods at any time before completion.

14. _F____

15. Under the bulk transfer law, the parties must prepare a schedule of the property being transferred so that it can be identified.

15. _____

58

Language of the Law

Select the legal term that best matches each definition.

a. auction with reserve *minimum price*
b. auction without reserve *Absolute*
c. bid
d. bulk transfer
e. contract to sell
f. firm offer

g. future goods
h. goods
i. merchant
j. open-price terms
k. output contract

l. requirements contract
m. sale
n. Uniform Commercial Code (UCC)
o. usage of trade

Answer

1. An agreement under which title to goods is to pass at some future time
2. An offer made at an auction
3. Goods that are not yet in existence or under the control of people
4. An agreement to sell all the goods a seller manufactures to a particular buyer
5. An auction where the auctioneer may withdraw the goods at any time before the completion of the sale
6. All things that are movable at the time of identification to the contract for sale
7. The passing of title from the seller to the buyer for a price
8. An agreement whereby a buyer agrees to buy "all the potatoes we need for our restaurant" from a particular seller
9. The body of law covering sales contracts that has been wholly or partially adopted in every state
10. A merchant's promise to hold an offer open, which must be in writing and requires no consideration

1. _____
2. _____
3. _g_____
4. _____

5. _A_____
6. _____
7. _____

8. _____

9. _____

10. _____

Applying the Law

1. Othmer agreed to buy a VCR from Sykes for $350. The agreement was oral and called for the full amount to be paid in cash the next day. Othmer later refused to buy the VCR. Was the agreement enforceable? Why or why not?

_____

_____

_____

2. Northern Sporting Goods sold its entire inventory of skis, bindings, and boots to Goodwin for $50,000. Several weeks later, Northern Sporting Goods became insolvent. Creditors, who knew nothing of the sale of the skis, demanded that Goodwin return all the items purchased. Must Goodwin meet this demand? Why or why not?

_____

_____

_____

3. Gregory agreed to buy an unframed oil painting from Burns for $489. Later, Gregory asked whether Burns would frame the painting at no additional cost. Burns agreed. Why wouldn't Gregory have to provide additional consideration to make Burns's added promise enforceable?

_____

_____

_____

4. West Coast Canning Company contracted to buy 1,600 tons of tuna from Rugby, who operated a tuna fishing fleet. Rugby's ships went to sea and began fishing for the tuna. Two weeks later, when the catch was completed, Rugby's fleet headed for the canning company's pier. Were the tuna in the ship's holds considered future goods at that time? Explain.

_____

_____

5. Modern Electronics agreed to manufacture a high-powered transmitter specially for Briggs, a ham radio operator. The design was so unusual that it was unlikely that anyone else would buy it. The contract price for the completed set was to be $3,500. When the work was finished, Briggs refused to make payment, stating that any sale of goods at that price had to be in writing. Was her argument correct? Why or why not?

_____

_____

6. Stewart selected a new moped at Harriet's Cycle Shop. The sales price was $897. The salesperson promised delivery the following afternoon, and Stewart agreed to make payment in full at that time. After the cycle was made ready for delivery, Stewart called the shop and said that the deal was off. Did Harriet's Cycle Shop have any legal right to damages? Explain.

_____

_____

7. Harrington Manufacturing Company, located in Michigan, ordered 250 tons of soft coal from Allegheny Mining Company, a Pennsylvania firm. The coal was to be delivered and paid for at Harrington's plant located in Ohio. Why would the law that governs this transaction be the same in each of the three states involved?

_____

_____

8. Greensboro Produce Company contracted with Thornton for 20 tons of green beans to be grown in Thornton's farm and delivered when ready for canning. At the time of their agreement, the seed had not yet been planted. Was this a sale? Why or why not?

_____

_____

9. Crescent Motors, a car dealer, wrote to Webster offering to sell him a Jaguar for $16,500 and agreeing to hold the offer open for one week. Three days later, before Webster accepted, Crescent Motors withdrew its offer. Was the company legally able to do this? Why or why not?

_____

_____

10. Helms was the highest bidder in an auction sale for an antique rolltop desk. The auction was posted to be "with reserve." The auctioneer refused to accept Helms's bid for the desk, saying that it was not high enough, and withdrew the desk from the sale. Helms demanded that her bid be accepted. Did the auctioneer have the right to withdraw the desk from the sale? Explain.

_____

_____

16 Title and Risk of Loss

Chapter Outline

16-1 Void and Voidable Title

A. Title is _____

_____

B. Void title is _____

_____

C. Voidable title means _____

_____

D. When goods are entrusted to a merchant who sells them to a third party, the third party receives _____

_____

16-2 Passage of Title and Risk of Loss

A. Once goods are identified, title passes to the buyer when _____

_____

B. In a shipment contract, both title and risk of loss pass _____

_____

C. In a destination contract, both title and risk of loss pass _____

_____

D. When the contract calls for the buyer to pick up the goods,
   1. title passes to the buyer _____

   _____

   2. risk of loss passes to a
      a. merchant seller, when _____

      _____

      b. nonmerchant seller, when _____

      _____

E. Title to fungible goods may pass _____

_____

F. When a document of title is used, both title and risk of loss pass _____

_____

G. The parties may enter into an agreement setting forth _____

_____

H. Title to goods revests in the seller when _____

_____

I. The international law does not address questions dealing with _____

_____

J. The rules governing the passage of risk of loss are addressed _____

_____

16-3 Sales with Right of Return

A. When goods are sold on approval, they remain the property of the seller until _____

_____

B. On a sale or return, title belongs to _____

_____

16-4 Insurable Interest

Buyers may insure goods the moment a _____

_____

Legal Concepts

For each statement, write T *in the answer column if the statement is true or* F *if the statement is false.*

Answer

1. Buyers of goods acquire whatever title their sellers have to the property.   1. _T_____
2. Anyone with voidable title to goods is not able to transfer good title to others.   2. _____
3. The owner of goods who entrusts them to a merchant retains title to the goods if the merchant sells them to someone else in the ordinary course of business.   3. _____
4. Before title can pass from the seller to the buyer, goods must be identified to the contract.   4. _____
5. In a shipment contract, risk of loss passes from the seller to the buyer when the goods are delivered to a carrier.   5. ~~F~~ T
6. When terms of shipment do not specify shipping point or destination, it is assumed to be f.o.b. (free on board) the place of destination.   6. _____
7. If the seller is a merchant, the risk of loss passes when the buyer tenders delivery if the contract calls for the buyer to pick up the goods.   7. _____
8. Title to fungible goods may pass without the necessity of separating goods sold from the bulk.   8. _____
9. When a document of title is used in a sales transaction, both title and risk of loss pass to the buyer when the document is delivered to the buyer.   9. _____
10. Parties may enter into an agreement setting forth the exact time that risk of loss passes from the seller to the buyer.   10. _____
11. When the seller sends goods to the buyer that do not meet the contract requirements and are therefore unacceptable, the risk of loss remains with the seller.   11. _____
12. Goods held by the buyer on approval are subject to the claims of the buyer's creditors.   12. _____
13. Goods held on sale or return must be returned at the seller's risk and expense.   13. _____
14. A person must have an insurable interest in certain property in order to place insurance on it.   14. _____
15. Both the buyer and the seller may have an insurable interest in goods that are identified to the contract.   15. _T_____

Language of the Law

Select the legal term that best matches each definition.

a. c.f.
b. c.i.f.
c. c.o.d.
d. destination contract
e. document of title
f. f.a.s. vessel

g. f.o.b.
h. f.o.b. the place of destination
i. f.o.b. the place of shipment
j. fungible goods

k. sale on approval
l. sale or return
m. shipment contract
n. voidable title
o. void title

Answer

1. Contracts under which title is transferred when the seller tenders the goods at the place of destination
2. Goods of which any unit is the equivalent of any like unit
3. A term that means "cash on delivery"
4. A term meaning "free alongside"
5. No title at all
6. A paper that proves that the person who possesses it is entitled to receive the goods named in the document
7. Title that may be voided by one of the parties if he or she elects to do so
8. A term meaning "free on board"
9. A sale that allows goods to be returned even though they conform to the contract and the goods are delivered primarily for resale
10. A term that indicates that goods will be transported free of charge to the place from which the goods are to be shipped

1. _d_____
2. _____
3. _____
4. _____
5. _O_____
6. _____
7. _N_____
8. _____
9. _____
10. _F_____

Applying the Law

1. Midwest Grain Co. sold 150,000 bushels of corn to Eastern Milling Co., giving Eastern a grain elevator receipt from elevator No. 281. While still in the elevator, the corn was destroyed by fire. Eastern argued that Midwest must assume the loss. Was Eastern correct? Why or why not?

_____

_____

_____

2. Acme Sales Co. sold Feldman, a consumer, a VCR for $299, promising that if she did not like the unit after one week she could return it and get her money back. If the unit suffered damage during that week, would the seller have to return Feldman's money? Why or why not?

_____

_____

_____

3. Goods were shipped to Calvin Company, terms f.o.b., c.o.d. Calvin owed $350 on the shipment, plus shipping charges. When notified of the arrival of the goods, Calvin demanded their delivery without payment of the amount due, stating that title to the goods passed to the company when shipped. Did Calvin have the right to the goods? Why or why not?

_____

_____

_____

4. Jefferson bought a piano from Hamlin Piano Company with a condition that it would be delivered. Hamlin loaded the piano into its truck, but the piano was damaged when the driver hit an abutment. Jefferson had selected the piano, paid for it, and had it tuned before it was taken from the shop. Did Hamlin or Jefferson suffer the risk of loss to the piano? Explain.

_____

_____

_____

5. Summer Sewing Machine Company agreed to deliver a sewing machine to Hopkins for a two-week trial. If Hopkins did not want to buy the machine, he agreed to notify the seller to come pick it up. The two weeks passed and Hopkins did not call the seller. After a month, he received a bill for $375, the price that Summer had stated to Hopkins. He refused to honor the bill, claiming that approval of the sale had never been given. Could Summer collect the $375? Why or why not?

_____

_____

_____

6. Knapp, through fraudulent means, persuaded Rigby to sell her an antique Chippendale mirror that had been in Rigby's family for generations. Knapp told Rigby that the mirror was of little value. Knapp then sold it to a museum for $2,500. Rigby demanded the return of the mirror from the museum, claiming that Knapp's title was voidable and the museum could not continue as the owner. Did Rigby win the case? Why or why not?

_____

_____

_____

7. Hume, who was not a merchant, agreed to sell his tractor to Warne for $1,500. Hume told Warne that it was available for him to pick up at any time. Warne paid for the tractor and said that he would pick it up the next day. A week later the tractor was stolen from Hume's property. It had not been picked up by Warne as agreed. Must Warne or Hume suffer the loss? Why?

_____

_____

_____

8. Livingston bought and paid for a new watch from a jewelry store. The seller agreed to keep the watch until it was convenient for Livingston to pick it up. Another clerk, uninformed of the transaction, sold the same watch to Hill. Would Livingston be able to claim the watch from Hill? Explain.

_____

_____

_____

9. Orton bought a guaranteed used car from Sanders Used-Car Sales. After he had driven the car for several months, the police charged him with driving a stolen vehicle. The car was confiscated and returned to the real owner, from whom it had been stolen six months earlier. Did Orton have rights to the car? Why or why not?

_____

_____

_____

10. Ward ordered heavy machinery from a company in Moline, Illinois. The machinery was shipped to Ward, terms f.o.b. Moline. En route to its destination in Los Angeles, the machinery was destroyed when the freight train derailed and caught fire. Ward refused to honor the bill for the machinery. Would he be required to pay for it? Explain.

_____

_____

_____

17 Warranties and Product Liability

Chapter Outline

17-1 Express Warranties

A. Express warranties arise in the following ways

1. _____
2. _____
3. _____

B. Under the Magnuson-Moss Warranty Act, when a written warranty is given to a consumer all of the following must be done

1. _____
2. _____
3. _____

17-2 Implied Warranties

A. To be merchantable, goods must at least

1. _____
2. _____
3. _____
4. _____
5. _____
6. _____

B. The warranty of fitness for a particular purpose arises when _____
_____

C. Other implied warranties may arise from _____
_____

D. Under international law, unless the parties agree otherwise, goods must

1. _____
2. _____
3. _____
4. _____

17-3 Warranty of Title

A. Whenever goods are sold, the seller warrants that the title _____
_____

B. Under international law, the seller must deliver _____
_____

17-4 Exclusion of Warranties

A. To exclude the implied warranty of merchantability _____
_____

B. To exclude the implied warranty of fitness for a particular purpose _____

_____

C. Implied warranties may also be excluded by _____

_____

D. Many states protect consumers by saying that _____

_____

E. By statute in some states, the handling of human blood is considered _____

_____

17-5 Duty to Notify Seller of Defective Product

To recover damages for breach of warranty, buyers of defective goods must notify

_____

_____

17-6 Privity Not Required

Under the Uniform Commercial Code (UCC), warranties extend to people who _____

_____

_____

17-7 Product Liability

A. Negligence may be defined as _____

_____

_____

B. Under the doctrine of strict liability, it is not necessary to prove _____

_____

Legal Concepts

For each statement, write T *in the answer column if the statement is true or* F *if the statement is false.*

Answer

1. Express warranties may be made by both merchant and nonmerchant sellers.   1. _____
2. An express warranty can be created without the use of formal words such as *guarantee*.   2. _____
3. Whenever a seller of goods makes a statement of fact about the goods to a buyer as part of a transaction, an implied warranty is created.   3. _____
4. Any description of the goods that is made part of the basis of the bargain creates an express warranty.   4. _____
5. The Magnuson-Moss Warranty Act applies only when written warranties are made voluntarily on nonconsumer products.   5. _____
6. An implied warranty is created when a sample is made part of the basis of the bargain.   6. _____
7. A full warranty is only conferred upon the original buyer of a product.   7. _____
8. To be merchantable, fungible goods must be of fair, average quality.   8. _____
9. A claim for breach of warranty of merchantability can be made only if a defect exists when the goods are purchased.   9. _____
10. An innocent purchaser of stolen goods may retain title to the goods.   10. _____
11. Implied warranties may be excluded by having buyers examine the goods or the sample.   11. _____
12. In some states, including Florida and Massachusetts, the procurement, processing, storage, and distribution of human blood is called a sale rather than a service.   12. _____
13. Failure of the buyer to notify the seller about defective goods within a reasonable time will prevent the buyer from receiving breach-of-warranty money damages.   13. _____
14. Injured parties are often more successful in bringing suit for breach of warranty of merchantability than in bringing suit for negligence.   14. _____
15. For recovery under the doctrine of strict liability, the party bringing suit must prove negligence on the part of the manufacturer or seller when injury results from a defective product.   15. _____

Language of the Law

Select the legal term that best matches each definition.

a. consequential damages
b. consumer products
c. express warranty
d. full warranty
e. implied warranty
f. limited warranty

g. negligence
h. product liability
i. punitive damages
j. strict liability
k. usage of trade
l. warranty

m. warranty of fitness for a
   particular purpose
n. warranty of
   merchantability
o. warranty of title

Answer

1. A written guaranty that does not meet all the requirements of a full warranty   1. _____

2. A written guaranty under which a defective product will be repaired without charge within a reasonable time after a complaint has been made about it   2. _____

3. Law under which an injured buyer may recover damages from either the manufacturer, seller, or supplier because of a product's unsafe condition   3. _____

4. The failure to exercise that degree of care that a reasonably prudent person would have exercised under the same circumstances   4. _____

5. An assurance by the seller of goods that the title is good and the transfer rightful   5. _____

6. A warranty created by an affirmation of fact, a description of the goods, or by a sample or model   6. _____

7. Damages that do not flow directly and immediately from an act   7. _____

8. Under this theory of law, manufacturers have the duty to design reasonably safe products   8. _____

9. A warranty that is given only when the seller is a merchant   9. _____

10. A warranty that comes about when the buyer relies on the seller's skill and judgment to select the goods   10. _____

Applying the Law

1. As Kaplan drove away from the dealership where she had just purchased a new car, the steering mechanism in the new car failed. The car swerved out of control, injuring three pedestrians. Would the injured pedestrians have a legal claim against the car manufacturer? Why or why not?

_____

2. Malone ordered a set of illustrated history books from Sterline Publishing Company. Samples shown by the publisher's representative were on the best grade of paper and were printed in brilliant colors. When the books arrived, Malone was disappointed by the weak coloring and the cheap paper used in production. For what reason did he have a right of action in this situation?

_____

3. Evans sold a painting to Beacom, saying that it was an original by a well-known nineteenth-century artist. Beacom found out afterward that the painting was a copy of the original. The seller refused to negotiate an adjustment. Did Beacom have a remedy against Evans for breach of warranty? Why or why not?

_____

4. Denby selected and bought a television antenna from Harper's TV and Supply Shop without seeking advice from the shop owner. The reception through the new antenna was very poor. Another model would have given perfect reception. Did the shop breach the implied warranty of fitness for a particular purpose? Explain.

_____

5. Zukas bought a new electric snowblower. A week later Zukas's son was injured while using the snowblower. The injury was caused by a defect in the product. The manufacturer maintained that its liability was to Zukas only, not to Zukas's son. Was the manufacturer's argument correct? Why or why not?

_____

_____

6. Manzi read the description of a sport coat in a brochure he received from a mail-order house. He ordered the sport coat, enclosing a check with the order. When the sport coat arrived, Manzi found that it was different from the one described in the brochure. Did the mail-order house breach a warranty in this transaction? Explain.

_____

_____

7. Codwise discovered that the time-set mechanism on her automatic coffee maker did not work the day she bought it from her local appliance store. Ten months later, Codwise notified the appliance store of the defect, and the store refused to remedy the situation. Did Codwise have a cause of action against the store? Why or why not?

_____

_____

8. Kelley needed a power lawn mower. The seller, a merchant, guaranteed that his machine was sharp and would do a good job on Kelley's lawn. Kelley was invited to try the machine out around the seller's shop. The motor ran perfectly, although there was no grass on which he could test its real efficiency. He bought the mower, but returned it the following day. According to Kelley, it would not cut the grass. The seller defended the sale by reminding Kelley of his examination of the machine. Could Kelley recover the money paid for the ineffective mower? Explain.

_____

_____

9. Bach worked as a machinist supervisor. Work done in the shop allowed only 0.0001 of an inch tolerance in machine drive shafts for aircraft engines. He bought a micrometer, telling the company the specifications needed in this work. A defect in the measuring instrument resulted in the loss of $10,000 in time and materials in the precision work supervised by Bach. Could Bach's company recover this loss through an action against the seller? Why or why not?

_____

_____

10. Vasquez contracted with Acme Heating Company for installation of a new gas-burning furnace. Vasquez selected the furnace desired, accepting no suggestions from Acme's heating engineer. The furnace operated as it was supposed to by the standards of the heating industry. It did not, however, heat the house. A larger furnace would have been satisfactory. Vasquez sued Acme Heating Company for breach of warranty of fitness for a particular purpose. Did Vasquez win the case? Why or why not?

_____

_____

18 Performance and Breach of the Sales Contract

Chapter Outline

18-1 Obligations of the Parties

A. The seller is obligated to _____

B. The buyer is obligated to _____

C. All parties must act _____

18-2 Tender of Performance

A. Tender is necessary in order to _____

_____

B. The seller's obligation to deliver the goods is on the condition that the buyer _____

_____

18-3 Buyer's Right to Inspect Goods

Except when goods are shipped c.o.d. or when the contract provides for payment against a document of title, the buyer has the right to inspect the goods _____

_____

18-4 Buyer's Rights and Duties Upon Delivery of Improper Goods

A. When defective goods or goods not of the kind specified in the contract are delivered, the buyer may elect to

1. _____

2. _____

3. _____

B. Merchant buyers have a duty after the rejection of goods to _____

_____

C. Acceptance of goods takes place when the buyer does any of the following

1. _____

2. _____

3. _____

4. _____

D. A buyer may revoke an acceptance if _____

E. Under international law, the buyer must _____

_____

18-5 Seller's Right to Cure Improper Tender

To cure an improper tender means to _____

_____

18-6 Breach of Contract

A. Under the UCC, when either party repudiates the contract before the time for performance, the injured party may _____

_____

B. When a buyer breaches a sales contract, the seller may

1. _____

2. _____

3. _____

4. _____

5. _____

6. _____

C. When a seller breaches a sales contract, the buyer may

1. _____

2. _____

3. _____

4. _____

5. _____

6. _____

D. In general, an action for breach of contract for sale must be commenced _____
_____

E. Under international law if delivery is late, the buyer must _____
_____

Legal Concepts

For each statement, write T *in the answer column if the statement is true or* F *if the statement is false.*

Answer

1. In a sales contract, only the seller is obligated to act in good faith.   1. _____
2. The court must enforce a contract that it finds to be unconscionable.   2. _____
3. The court often looks at the usage of trade to supplement the express terms of a contract.   3. _____
4. The buyer is not obligated to pay for goods if the seller has not made tender of delivery.   4. _____
5. Tender of delivery must be made at a reasonable hour of the day.   5. _____
6. The seller has no right to demand payment in legal tender.   6. _____
7. Legally, a contract for the sale of goods may never require payment before inspection of the goods delivered.   7. _____
8. When defective goods are delivered, the buyer may accept any commercial unit and reject the rest.   8. _____
9. A merchant must make a reasonable effort to sell rejected perishable goods.   9. _____
10. A revocation of acceptance is not effective until the buyer notifies the seller of it.   10. _____
11. The seller always has the right to cure nonconforming goods.   11. _____
12. When either party to a sales contract repudiates the contract before the time for performance, the injured party must wait until the actual time for performance before bringing suit.   12. _____
13. Both incidental and consequential damages may not be awarded in the same case.   13. _____
14. When improper goods are delivered, the buyer may keep them and ask the seller for an adjustment.   14. _____
15. Lawsuits have a time limit within which suit must be brought.   15. _____

Language of the Law

Select the legal term that best matches each definition.

a. anticipatory breach
b. carrier
c. commercial unit
d. cover
e. cure

f. insolvent
g. legal tender
h. liquidated damages
i. specific performance
j. stoppage in transit

k. tender of delivery
l. tender of payment
m. tender of performance
n. unconscionable contract
o. writ of replevin

Answer

1. The remedy of buying similar goods from someone else and suing the seller for the difference between the agreed price and the cost of the purchase

1. _____

2. That which occurs when the parties to a contract for sale offer to do that which they have agreed to do

2. _____

3. A contract that is oppressively one-sided, giving unfair advantage to one of the parties

3. _____

4. The act by the seller of offering to turn the goods over to the buyer

4. _____

5. A single whole for the purpose of a sale

5. _____

6. The exact amount due in U.S. currency

6. _____

7. A decree granted by a court of equity that requires the seller to deliver unique or rare goods described in the sales agreement to the buyer

7. _____

8. The act of the buyer of offering to turn the money over to the seller

8. _____

9. A court action used to require the seller to convey identified goods to the purchaser who has been unable to obtain the goods elsewhere

9. _____

10. The right of a seller to have the delivery of goods stopped before they reach their destination

10. _____

Applying the Law

1. Fantini Baking Co. ordered 1,000 bushels of Baldwin apples from Groveland Orchards for use in making apple pies. By mistake, Groveland Orchards shipped Mac-Intosh apples, which Fantini could not use. Could Fantini allow the MacIntosh apples to rot while it waited for Groveland to correct the error? Explain.

_____

_____

_____

2. Eye Care Outlet entered into a contract to buy 1,000 eyeglass frames from Weeks. The frames were to be delivered on October 15. On June 15, four months before the delivery date, Eye Care notified Weeks that it was canceling the order. Could Weeks bring suit immediately against Eye Care Outlet for breach of contract? Why or why not?

_____

_____

_____

3. Style Rite Furniture Company ordered eight complete bedroom sets from National Furniture Supply Company. When one of the beds was found to be broken, Style Rite rejected not only the broken bed but also the rest of the pieces in that particular set of furniture. Was Style Rite's rejection legal? Why or why not?

_____

_____

4. Rousette signed an agreement to buy an antique mirror of unusual design from Amirault, who agreed in writing to deliver it in one week. Two days later, the seller telephoned Rousette, saying that she had decided to keep the mirror for her own personal use because of its rarity. She assured Rousette that she would return his deposit in full. Could Rousette bring an action against Amirault to receive the mirror? Explain.

---

5. Tiny Tots Toy Company entered into a contract with Superior Electric Train Company for the purchase of 100 electric train sets. By mistake, the train sets were delivered to Tiny Tim's Toy Company. Nevertheless, when billed for the trains, Tiny Tots paid for them, not realizing the error. Five years later, when its books were audited in preparation for a computerized accounting system, Tiny Tots discovered that it had not received the electric train sets. Could Tiny Tots recover damages from Superior Electric Train Company for failing to deliver the goods? Why or why not?

---

6. Davis, who had lost her job and was on welfare, was approached by a fast-talking salesperson one afternoon as she was sweeping off her front sidewalk. After discussing her difficulties of being out of a job and relying on welfare to support her five children, the salesperson talked her into signing a contract to install aluminum siding on her small bungalow for $20,000. Later that day, Davis learned from a neighbor that such a job was worth no more than $2,000. On what grounds might Davis be able to have the contract declared void?

---

7. Sanborn ordered a leather jacket from the Amesbury Leather Company, which agreed to ship the jacket to Sanborn c.o.d. When the jacket was delivered, Sanborn insisted that she be allowed to inspect it before paying for it. Did she have the right to do so? Explain.

---

8. Vaughn Corporation sent one of its employees to pick up some parts it had ordered from Valley Supply Company. The employee offered to pay for the parts with a Vaughn Corporation check made payable to Valley Supply for the correct amount. Valley Supply refused to take the check, saying that it had to have cash before it could release the goods. Was Valley Supply within its rights? Why or why not?

---

9. Meehan agreed to sell 500 cases of canned vegetables to Katz for $3,500, f.o.b. Katz's warehouse. Meehan refused to deliver the goods, however, until he received payment, and Katz would not pay for the goods until they were delivered. Meehan sued Katz for breach of contract. Would Meehan win the case? Why or why not?

---

10. Lenz agreed to buy McIsaac's secondhand Ferrari automobile, although it did not run, upon being assured by McIsaac that the parts to make it run had been ordered and would arrive within a month. McIsaac promised to put the car in running order when the parts arrived. Lenz paid for the car and had it towed to her property. Three months later, the parts still had not arrived, and the car sat idle, unable to be used. Could Lenz legally return the car to McIsaac? Give a reason for your answer.

---

19 Consumer Protection

Chapter Outline

19-1 Consumer Protection Laws

Consumer protection laws apply to transactions entered into between _____
_____

19-2 The Federal Trade Commission (FTC) Act

The FTC Act states that _____
_____

19-3 The FTC Rules

A. The Used Car Rule requires used car dealers to _____
_____

B. Under the Door-to-Door Sales Rule, sales of consumer goods or services over _____
_____

C. Under the Mail Order Rule, sellers must _____
_____

D. Telemarketing fraud includes get-rich-quick schemes involving _____
_____

E. Some 900-number scams may disclose _____
_____

F. While some work-at-home plans are legitimate, _____
_____

19-4 Unfair or Deceptive Acts or Practices

A. People who receive unordered merchandise through the mail may _____
_____

B. The purpose of bait advertising is to _____

C. The Federal Odometer Law prohibits people from _____
_____

19-5 Consumer Product Safety Act

The Consumer Product Safety Act was passed to protect consumers from _____
_____

19-6 Consumer Leasing Act

The Consumer Leasing Act requires leasing companies to _____
_____

19-7 Consumer Credit Laws

A. Under the Truth-in-Lending Act, lenders must disclose to borrowers

   1. _____   2. _____

B. Under the Equal Credit Opportunity Act, people who apply for credit may not be
asked _____

C. Under the Truth-in-Lending Act, credit cardholders are not responsible for _____

_____

D. Under the Fair Credit Reporting Act, consumers have the right to know _____

_____

E. The Fair Credit Billing Act establishes a procedure for _____

F. The Fair Debt Collection Practices Act was passed to prevent _____

_____

19-8 Food, Drug, and Cosmetic Act

Consumers are protected by the Food, Drug, and Cosmetic Act against _____

_____

19-9 Fair Packaging and Labeling Act

A. Labels must indicate

1. _____   2. _____

3. _____   4. _____

B. Beginning in 1992, the FDA regulations required _____

_____

Legal Concepts

For each statement, write T *in the answer column if the statement is true or* F *if the statement is false.*

Answer

1. People who buy or rent things from a consumer for business use are protected by consumer protection laws.

2. State consumer protection offices help to enforce state consumer protection laws and provide information.

3. The FTC Act applies to all intrastate commerce.

4. Under the Used Car Rule, the Buyer's Guide must post a statement listing the specific systems that are covered by the warranty.

5. Under the Door-to-Door Sales Rule, sales of consumer goods or services made at a customer's home may be cancelled within three business days if the price of the sale is more than $25.

6. Consumers who order goods by mail must receive either their goods or an option notice within 60 days.

7. Failure to disclose important facts about a product is not a deceptive or unfair act.

8. People who receive unordered merchandise through the mail must return it to the sender.

9. It is illegal to disconnect or reset the odometer of a motor vehicle.

10. The Consumer Product Safety Act covers products or component parts manufactured or distributed for sale for personal use or enjoyment and includes coverage of motor vehicles.

11. The Consumer Leasing Act applies to daily rentals of personal property for personal, family, or household use.

12. Under the Truth-in-Lending Act, lenders must disclose both the finance charge and the annual percentage rate.

13. People who apply for credit may legally be asked whether they are divorced or widowed.

14. Under the Truth-in-Lending Act, credit cardholders are responsible for the first $100 only of any unauthorized charges.

15. The Food and Drug Administration (FDA) has the power to regulate cosmetic products and medical devices such as mechanical hearts.

1. _____

2. _____

3. _____

4. _____

5. _____

6. _____

7. _____

8. _____

9. _____

10. _____

11. _____

12. _____

13. _____

14. _____

15. _____

74

Name _____ Date _____

Language of the Law

Select the legal term that best matches each definition.

a. annual percentage rate
b. bait-and-switch scheme
c. balloon payment
d. Buyer's Guide
e. closed-end credit

f. *cognovits*
g. consent order
h. consumer
i. finance charge
j. interstate commerce

k. intrastate commerce
l. open-end credit
m. punitive damages
n. revolving charge account
o. Used Car Rule

Answer

1. Insincere offers to sell a product that the advertiser does not intend to sell
2. The actual cost of a loan in dollars and cents
3. An account that may have an outstanding balance at all times
4. A way in which the FTC may cause a company to stop a disputed practice without making the company admit to any guilt
5. A person who buys or rents things from a business for personal use
6. Business activity that involves more than one state
7. An informative sticker placed in the window of a used car offered for sale
8. Credit that is extended for a specific amount of money only
9. Local business activity carried on within state boundaries
10. The true rate of interest on a loan

1. _____
2. _____
3. _____

4. _____
5. _____
6. _____
7. _____
8. _____
9. _____
10. _____

Applying the Law

1. Forsyth ordered some printed stationery from a mail-order firm, enclosing a check in payment. After waiting 45 days and receiving no response, Forsyth canceled the order and demanded the return of her money. Was Forsyth within her rights? Explain.

_____

_____

_____

2. Tin Kee Ng, a single parent of three children, applied for credit at a local department store. The store manager refused the credit application because Ng was receiving welfare payments. Could Ng challenge the store's refusal to extend credit? Why or why not?

_____

_____

3. Guzman, who lived in New Jersey, bought a stereo cabinet from a dealer while visiting friends in North Carolina. She paid for the cabinet with a credit card, and the dealer agreed to ship it to her home in New Jersey. The cabinet that arrived in New Jersey displayed defective workmanship, and the credit card issuer refused to adjust Guzman's bill. Was Guzman entitled to relief under the Fair Credit Billing Act? Explain.

_____

_____

4. Conway went to an appliance store to buy a refrigerator that was advertised in the newspaper. The salesperson discouraged her from buying the advertised refrigerator, saying that it was small, of poor quality, and not self-defrosting. The salesperson tried to talk Conway into buying a more expensive refrigerator of better quality. Did the salesperson violate the law? Explain.

_____

_____

5. Blair sold his three-year-old car to Wilson. Two years earlier, when the car's odometer had malfunctioned after running 7,000 miles, Blair had installed a new odometer, which was set at zero miles. On the bill of sale to Wilson, Blair disclosed the present mileage reading. Did Blair violate the law? Explain.

_____

_____

_____

6. Carlucci applied for and received a Chevron credit card from the Chevron Oil Company. Shortly after the card was received, it was stolen and used for the unauthorized purchase of gasoline, tires, and a battery, totaling $274.49. Carlucci refused to pay Chevron for the merchandise purchased with the stolen card, although his responsibility was set forth in the notice received when the card was delivered by mail. Was Carlucci responsible for all of the unauthorized purchases that were made on the stolen card? Why or why not?

_____

_____

_____

7. Romano signed a contract for the purchase of a $4,000 above-ground pool and accessories sold to him by a sales representative who visited all the homes in the neighborhood. Romano made a $300 down payment and agreed to pay the balance in monthly installments of $112. After the sales representative departed, Romano realized that the monthly payments were more than he could safely afford. The following morning Romano wrote to the supplier stating that he wished to cancel the agreement. Could this contract be canceled? Why or why not?

_____

_____

_____

8. Ley had been turned down for credit by several commercial establishments before discovering that the refusals were prompted by a bad credit report furnished by a credit bureau. Ley went to the credit bureau's office and demanded to see the contents of his file, but met with a refusal. Ley filed suit under the Fair Credit Reporting Act in the federal district court for willful noncompliance. Ley sought $300 in actual damages for claimed lost wages and $25,000 in punitive damages. The credit bureau asked the court to throw out the suit, asserting that Ley's actual damages were imaginary and that punitive damages could not be awarded without proof of actual damages. Why might the court deny the credit bureau's motion for dismissal?

_____

_____

_____

9. A gasoline credit card was mailed to Jacoby, although she had not applied for it. The card was stolen from her mailbox and unauthorized purchases amounting to $260 were made. Would Jacoby be liable for any of the purchases made on the unsolicited gasoline credit card? Why or why not?

_____

_____

_____

10. Riley signed a retail installment sales contract with a local merchant that covered the purchase of a solid-state console color television. The merchant sold the installment note to a third-party creditor in order to obtain cash. When the television failed to operate reliably, Riley refused to make any further payments. Could Riley discontinue payments while seeking redress for failure of the television to operate properly? Explain.

_____

_____

_____

_____

76

20 Personal Property and Bailments

Chapter Outline

20-1 Personal Property

A. The finder of lost property has a legal responsibility to _____

_____

B. The three requirements for a transfer to be considered a gift are

1. _____

2. _____

3. _____

C. Under the Uniform Transfers to Minors Act (UTMA), minors are assured _____

_____

D. A thief acquires _____

_____

20-2 Intellectual Property

A. A patent gives the owner the exclusive right to _____

_____

B. To be legally protected, a patented item must _____

_____

C. The transfer of a patent is accomplished by _____

_____

D. Under the Paris Convention for the Protection of Industrial Property, each country

guarantees _____

_____

_____

E. Under the copyright law, works are protected for _____

_____

F. Trademarks can be established in three different ways

1. _____

2. _____

3. _____

G. Companies can lose their trademark protection if _____

_____

20-3 Bailments of Personal Property

A bailment is the _____

_____

20-4 Principal Types of Bailments

The principal types of bailments are

A. _____

	B.	_____
	C.	_____

20-5 Bailments Imposed by Law

A. In an involuntary bailment, personal property is _____

B. The finder of lost property is considered to be the _____

20-6 Duties of Bailor and Bailee

A. The bailor must deliver _____

B. Under modern theory, the duty of all bailees is to exercise _____

20-7 Tortious Bailees

The four types of tortious bailees are

A. _____

B. _____

C. _____

D. _____

Legal Concepts

For each statement, write T *in the answer column if the statement is true or* F *if the statement is false.*

Answer

1. All personal property has substance that can be touched.
1. *F*

2. Money due on a note or contract is not personal property.
2. _____

3. The finder of lost property has a legal responsibility to make an effort to learn the identity of the owner and return the property to that person.
3. _____

4. Under the UTMA, the custodianship terminates when the minor reaches the age of 18.
4. _____

5. Under the UTMA, the income from a gift to a minor over the age of 14 is taxable to the minor rather than to the person who gave the gift.
5. _____

6. A thief acquires title to goods that are stolen and therefore can convey a good title to someone else.
6. _____

7. A patent may be obtained if the subject matter of the patent would be obvious to a person having ordinary skill in the field.
7. _____

8. Under common law, trademarks may be established by usage rather than by registration with the state or federal government.
8. _____

9. When a bailment relationship ends, the bailee must return to the bailor the same goods as were delivered and accepted.
9. _____

10. The surrender of car keys to a parking lot or garage attendant is a sufficient delivery of possession and control to create a bailment.
10. _____

11. Agreements in which property is transferred to another for repairs for which the owner agrees to pay a fee are bailments for the sole benefit of the bailee.
11. _____

12. A trademark registration remains in force for 25 years.
12. *F*

13. By implication, the finder of lost property becomes the bailee of the article if he or she takes possession of it.
13. _____

14. In a bailment for the sole benefit of the bailor, the bailee has an implied right to use the bailor's property.
14. _____

15. Tortious bailees are responsible for any damage that results to property in their possession regardless of the cause of the damage.
15. _____

Language of the Law

Select the legal term that best matches each definition.

a. bailee
b. bailment by necessity
c. bailment for the sole benefit of the bailee
d. bailment for the sole benefit of the bailor
e. bailor
f. copyright
g. donee
h. donor
i. gift *in causa mortis*
j. gratuitous bailment
k. involuntary bailment
l. *mutuum*
m. personal property
n. tortious bailee
o. trademark

		Answer
1.	The type of mutual-benefit bailment created when a customer gives up possession of a hat while getting a haircut	1. B
2.	Any word, name, symbol, or device adopted and used by a manufacturer to identify goods and distinguish them from those sold by others	2. O
3.	The person who gives a gift	3. H
4.	A transaction in which borrowed goods are replaced with an equal quantity of the same goods	4. L
5.	The owner of the property involved in a bailment	5. E
6.	A bailment that lacks consideration by either party	6. J
7.	A person who has wrongful possession of another's goods	7. N
8.	A gift given by someone in anticipation of his or her own death from a known cause	8. I
9.	Legal rights that protect the writings of authors and the works of artists from unauthorized reproduction	9. F
10.	Everything that can be owned other than real estate	10. M

Applying the Law

1. Smith, fearing death from severe injuries suffered in an automobile accident, gave his friend an expensive gold watch. Smith recovered from his injuries. Must the friend give the watch back if Smith wants it back? Why or why not?

_____
_____
_____

2. Stephanie Gregory, who was six years old, received a gift of $2,000 from her grandfather, who followed the procedures established by the UTMA. Was the interest earned on Stephanie's bank account taxable to Stephanie's parents? Explain.

_____
_____
_____

3. Kimball left her pocketbook on a chair beside the table in the restaurant where she had dinner. St. Pierre, the next customer of the restaurant who sat at that table, discovered the pocketbook and told the manager about it. The manager allowed St. Pierre to keep the pocketbook. Kimball contends that the manager violated the law. Was Kimball correct? Why or why not?

_____
_____
_____

4. Tubbs found a gold watch in an airport waiting room. There was nothing to identify the watch. Tubbs put it in his pocket, satisfied that "finders keepers, losers weepers" was the law. Was Tubbs correct? Explain.

_____

_____

5. Evans stopped at her hairstylist by appointment. The operator asked her to leave her hat on a rack outside the operating booth. When Evans was ready to leave, the hat was gone. The manager denied liability, pointing to a sign reading, "Not Responsible for Personal Property." Was the hair stylist responsible for the loss? Explain.

_____

_____

6. During a windstorm, a neighbor's folding chairs blew into Miller's yard. Miller disliked the neighbor and threw the chairs into the street, where they were crushed by a truck. Could Miller be held liable for the neighbor's loss? Why or why not?

_____

_____

7. Sanchez used a distinctive trademark on boxes of candy he made and sold locally. A competitor, Russo, copied and used the trademark on boxes of popcorn that she sold locally. Sanchez claimed that he was protected by the federal trademark laws. Was he correct? Why or why not?

_____

_____

8. Mueller attended the Army-Navy football game in Philadelphia. Kovich loaned Mueller a pair of binoculars to make the game more interesting. The binoculars were stolen when Mueller left them on a vacant seat during halftime. Was Mueller liable for damages for the loss? Give a reason for your answer.

_____

_____

9. Kinkaid asked permission to put a car in Anderson's two-car garage during a heavy snowstorm. After Kinkaid put the car in, Anderson locked the garage door, taking the key into the house. Kinkaid's car was stolen from the garage, but Anderson's was left untouched by the thieves. Was Anderson liable to Kinkaid for the loss of the car? Explain.

_____

_____

10. Harris rented a boat from Dukes for a trip to an island located two miles offshore. Since it was a good day for sailing, Harris continued the trip 50 miles farther across the bay. During that part of the trip, the boat struck a submerged piling, ripping out the bottom and ruining the craft. Harris proved in court that the accident did not result from any lack of care nor was it caused by any negligent act. Was Harris responsible to Dukes for the loss? Why or why not?

_____

_____

_____

21 Innkeepers, Carriers, and Warehousers

Chapter Outline

21-1 Innkeepers

A. An innkeeper has an obligation to accept _____
_____

    1. The Civil Rights Act of 1964 prohibits _____
_____

    2. People may be turned away when _____
_____

B. In protecting guests from harm, innkeepers must use _____

C. Innkeepers have a lien on _____

21-2 Carriers

A. Contract carriers are permitted by law to _____
_____

B. Common carriers are liable as insurers of goods except in the case of

    1. _____

    2. _____

    3. _____

    4. _____

    5. _____

C. Common carriers may refuse goods that

    1. _____

    2. _____

    3. _____

    4. _____

    5. _____

D. Common carriers may enforce the following rights against shippers:

    1. _____

    2. _____

E. Common carriers may refuse passengers when

    1. _____

    2. _____

F. Airline passengers who are eligible for denied boarding compensation must be offered _____

G. For travel wholly within the United States, the maximum liability of an airline for lost luggage is _____

A. A public warehouser is _____

_____

B. A private warehouser is _____

_____

C. A warehouser must use that amount of care that _____

_____

D. A warehouser's lien is _____

Legal Concepts

For each statement, write T *in the answer column if the statement is true or* F *if the statement is false.*

Answer

1. An innkeeper, with some exceptions, is required to accept all guests who apply for accommodation.

1. _____

2. Hotel guests are not guaranteed by law the exclusive and undisturbed privacy of their assigned rooms.

2. _____

3. A hotel may discriminate racially in selecting guests.

3. __F____

4. Innkeepers are permitted a right of lien on the property of a guest.

4. _____

5. With exceptions, innkeepers are held by law to be insurers of their guests' property.

5. _____

6. Contract carriers are required to operate on regular schedules.

6. _____

7. Intrastate carriers and private carriers are regulated by the Interstate Commerce Commission (ICC).

7. _____

8. Common carriers of goods are insurers of all goods accepted for shipment.

8. __T____

9. A common carrier is relieved of liability for damages resulting from mob violence.

9. _____

10. A common carrier does not have the right to discriminate in selection of passengers carried.

10. _____

11. Throughout the last decade, there has been a strong trend toward more government regulation of the transportation industry.

11. _____

12. Warehousers are mutual-benefit bailees.

12. _____

13. A warehouser must use a reasonable amount of care to avoid being charged with negligence.

13. _____

14. Fungible goods may not be commingled by a warehouser.

14. _____

15. If goods are not removed from a warehouse at the end of a storage period, the warehouser may sell them after giving proper notice.

15. _____

Language of the Law

Select the legal term that best matches each definition.

a. commingled
b. common carrier
c. consignee
d. consignor
e. contract carrier
f. demurrage charge
g. innkeeper
h. lien
i. order bill of lading
j. passenger
k. private carrier
l. transient
m. warehouse receipt
n. warehouser
o. warehouser's lien

Answer

1. Companies not in the transportation business that operate their own trucks and other vehicles to transport their own goods

1. _____

2. A guest whose length of stay is variable

2. _____

3. A claim that one has against the property of another

3. _____

4. A carrier that provides transportation for compensation only to those with whom it chooses to do business

4. _____

5. Mixed together   5. _____
6. An additional fee charged for extended storage of goods   6. _____
7. A receipt issued by a party engaged in the business of storing goods for hire 7. _____
8. The right to retain possession of warehoused goods until satisfaction of the charges
   imposed upon them   8. _____
9. The party shipping goods under a bill of lading   9. _____
10. A person engaged in the business of storing goods for hire   10. _____

Applying the Law

1. Grady, a guest at the Wayside Motel, was unable to pay the motel bill. The motel manager took Grady's luggage, saying that Grady could have it back when the bill was paid. What rule of law allowed the manager to take this action?

_____

_____

2. Most of the goods contained in a freight train (a common carrier) were ruined when a tornado wrecked the train. The carrier was sued for damages by all the shippers under the carrier's obligation as an insurer of the freight. Was the carrier liable? Why or why not?

_____

_____

_____

3. McKay picked up the goods that he had stored in Dexter's warehouse, promising to pay Dexter the following week. Several months passed, and McKay still had not paid Dexter for storing the goods. Dexter claimed that he had a warehouser's lien on the goods that were stored in his warehouse. Was Dexter correct? Explain.

_____

_____

_____

4. Petrocelli checked luggage at the reservations counter on East-West Airlines, a common carrier. Upon arrival in St. Louis, she presented the baggage check. An airline attendant could not find the luggage. Was East-West Airlines liable to Petrocelli? Why or why not?

_____

_____

_____

5. Sheridan entered the Clark Hotel intoxicated and used profanity in the presence of several registered guests. The room clerk then refused to accept him as a guest. Sheridan sued the hotel for failure to accept him. Would Sheridan win the case? Explain.

_____

_____

_____

6. Hall, who had made reservations six months in advance, was told when she arrived at the airport that she had been bumped. The airline agent told her that the airlines had asked for volunteers to give up their reservations but no one had done so; thus, Hall had no recourse. Was the airline agent correct? Explain.

_____

_____

7. Ohio and Western Railroad, a common carrier, accepted goods for shipment to the Keen Company in Illinois. Freight charges were to be collected from Keen. Keen demanded the goods without payment of the charges. Did the railroad have to accede to Keen's demands? Why or why not?

_____

_____

8. Walker, a bus passenger, was injured when a tire blew out, causing the bus to turn over. It was proved that the tire was a new one that had been mounted on the bus only the day before. Was the carrier liable to Walker for his injuries? Explain.

_____

_____

9. Cleaver retired for the night in the Clairmont Hotel. Ignoring a notice posted in the room, Cleaver did not leave his watch and ring at the hotel desk for safekeeping during the night. Both items were stolen by an intruder. Could the hotel be held responsible for these losses? Why or why not?

_____

_____

10. While staying at the Centerville Hotel, Williams was injured when an elevator dropped two floors to the basement. The elevator had been carefully checked by competent technicians only one hour before the accident. Was the hotel liable for Williams's injuries? Explain.

_____

_____

22 Real Property

Chapter Outline

22-1 The Nature of Real Property

A. Landowners now own the airspace up to as high as _____
_____

B. Under the riparian rights doctrine, landowners _____
_____

C. Under the prior appropriation doctrine, the first person _____

D. In deciding whether or not an item is a fixture, the courts ask
  1. _____
  2. _____
  3. _____
  4. _____

22-2 Easements

A. An easement may be created
  1. _____
  2. _____
  3. _____

B. An easement by prescription is _____
_____
_____

22-3 Estates in Real Property

A. The holder of an estate in fee simple has _____
_____

B. A life estate may be created
  1. _____
  2. _____
  3. _____

22-4 Co-Ownership of Real Property

A. When a tenant in common dies, his or her share passes _____
_____

B. Four unities required to create a joint tenancy are
  1. _____
  2. _____
  3. _____
  4. _____

C. Upon the death of one joint tenant, the entire ownership _____
_____

D. A tenancy by the entirety may be held only by _____

22-5 Methods of Acquiring Title to Real Property

A. Types of deeds

    1. A general warranty deed guarantees _____

    _____

    2. A special warranty deed guarantees _____

    _____

    3. A bargain-and-sale deed is one that _____

    _____

    4. A quitclaim deed is one that _____

    _____

B. When people die owning real property solely, title passes _____

C. To establish adverse possession, claimants must prove

    1. _____

    2. _____

    3. _____

    4. _____

22-6 Zoning Laws

Zoning laws protect against _____

22-7 Eminent Domain

Eminent domain is the right _____

Legal Concepts

For each statement, write T *in the answer column if the statement is true or* F *if the statement is false.*

Answer

1. Real property does not include perennial plants.

   1. _____

2. Someone who owns land has the right to cut off trespassing tree branches and roots that intrude into that land from another person's property.

   2. _____

3. Air rights are valuable and sometimes become a tax source for the government.

   3. _____

4. If a stream is navigable, the owner on each side owns from his or her bank to the center of the stream.

   4. _____

5. A built-in stove and an under-the-counter dishwasher are considered personal property.

   5. _____

6. Once an easement is created, it is bought and sold with the land.

   6. _T_

7. A person who has a freehold estate may transfer that interest to another by sale, gift, will, or dying without a will.

   7. _T_

8. The most common form of ownership of real property is a life estate.

   8. _F_

9. When two or more people own real property as tenants in common, one cotenant's interest is always the same as each of the other cotenants' interests.

   9. _____

10. Upon the death of one of the parties who own real property as tenants by the entirety, no administration of the estate is necessary to give clear title to the survivor.

   10. _____

11. A deed becomes effective when it is delivered by the grantee to the grantor.

   11. _____

12. A quitclaim deed is the most desirable form of deed from the point of view of the grantee.

   12. _F_

13. When someone dies with a will, title to their real property passes to the persons named in the will without the use of a deed.

   13. _____

14. Newly passed zoning laws do not apply to existing uses of land.

   14. _____

15. Zoning laws help to keep property values from declining and protect against the undesirable use of neighboring property.

15. _____

Language of the Law

Select the legal term that best matches each definition.

a. adverse possession
b. curtesy
c. dower
d. easement
e. eminent domain
f. grantee
g. grantor
h. life estate
i. quitclaim deed
j. real property
k. riparian owners
l. special warranty deed
m. tenancy by the entirety
n. tenants in common
o. variance

Answer

1. A deed that transfers to the buyer only the interest that the seller may have in a property

1. *I*

2. An exemption or an exception permitting a use of property that differs from the uses permitted under the existing zoning ordinance

2. *O*

3. The right of federal, state, and local governments to take private lands for public use by compensating the owners for the land taken

3. *E*

4. The ground and everything permanently attached to it

4. *J*

5. People who own land along the bank of a river or stream

5. *K*

6. The right of a landowner to use the real property of another in a limited way

6. *D*

7. A tenancy based on the common law that may be held only by a husband and wife

7. *M*

8. A common law right of a wife to a one-third life estate in real property owned by her husband upon his death

8. *C*

9. Ownership of real property for one's life or for the life of another

9. *H*

10. The person to whom title in real property is transferred by deed

10. *F*

Applying the Law

1. Gregory owned an ultralight airplane. She flew the plane 300 feet above the surface of some land owned by a neighbor, Brown. When Brown complained, Gregory argued that she was flying in the navigable air space. Was Gregory correct? Explain.

_____

_____

2. LaPlant owned a life estate in Stillwater Farm. When she moved to a nursing home, LaPlant said to her daughter, "You may stay at Stillwater Farm for as long as you live." Were LaPlant's instructions to her daughter accurate? Why or why not?

_____

_____

3. Conrad owned, individually, a vacation cottage in the mountains. When Conrad died, his son, Andrew, inherited the property. Andrew claimed that he did not have good title because he had no deed to the property. Was Andrew correct? Explain.

_____

_____

4. Waverly, whose house was situated behind Southwick's house, had a recorded easement to use a driveway through Southwick's land. When Waverly sold the house, Southwick tried to stop the new owner from using the driveway. Was Southwick successful in doing so? Explain.

_____

_____

_____

5. Richards's water supply came from an artesian well that had been drilled to a point 89 feet below the surface of his land. A nearby water company drilled wells to a much deeper depth on its property. Thousands of gallons of water were pumped out each day to provide water to buyers a mile away. Richards's well went dry because of the water company's lowering of the depth of available percolating waters. For what legal reason can he succeed in enjoining the water company from such use as has interfered with the water rights to his property?

_____

_____

_____

6. Starrett beautified a property by planting several hundred flower bulbs, shrubs, and perennials. The property was sold to Hawthorne. Before giving up possession of the property, Starrett began digging out the bulbs and other plantings. It was her plan to move them all to a new home that she had bought. Could Hawthorne stop her from taking these plants? Why or why not?

_____

_____

_____

7. Rudner owned property through which Red Clay Creek flowed. Greenbank Mills, upstream from the Rudner property, started discharging waste chemicals into the creek. Rudner complained of the obnoxious odor and discoloration of the usually clear, clean water in the stream. Would Rudner succeed in restricting Greenbank's use of Red Clay Creek? Why or why not?

_____

_____

_____

8. Rheinhold and Kruger owned adjoining farms. The limbs of a large apple tree on Kruger's farm spread over Rheinhold's land, and its roots grew into Rheinhold's soil. Rheinhold cut off the limbs and the roots that extended onto his property. Could Kruger recover damages from Rheinhold in court? Explain.

_____

_____

9. The sprawling plant of United Smelter Corporation required the lands of a neighbor to allow necessary expansion for growth. The board of directors voted to initiate eminent-domain proceedings to get the land. Would this action be permitted? Explain.

_____

_____

_____

10. Haggert owned a condominium at Ocean Shores. The main air-conditioning unit for the building had to be replaced. Haggert refused to share in the expense, saying that he owned only his unit. For what legal reason did Haggert have an ownership interest in a part of the condominium other than his own unit?

_____

_____

_____

88

23 Landlord and Tenant

Chapter Outline

23-1 Landlord-Tenant Relationships

The elements necessary for the creation of the landlord-tenant relationship are

A. _____

B. _____

C. _____

D. _____

E. _____

23-2 Leasing Versus Other Relationships

A. A lease differs from a license in that _____

_____

B. A lodger is _____

23-3 Types of Leasehold Interests

A. A tenancy at will is _____

B. A tenancy for years is _____

C. A periodic tenancy is _____

D. A tenancy at sufferance arises _____

_____

23-4 The Lease Agreement

A. The essential requirements of a lease are

1. _____

2. _____

3. _____

B. Security deposits protect _____

C. An option to renew gives _____

_____

D. An option to purchase is _____

_____

E. An assignment of a lease occurs when _____

_____

F. A sublease occurs when _____

23-5 Rights and Duties of Landlords and Tenants

A. Landlords may not discriminate in selecting tenants on the grounds of _____

_____

B. The warranty of habitability means _____

_____

_____

C. The landlord has the following rights

    1. _____

    2. _____

    3. _____

D. The tenant is entitled to _____

_____

E. Tenants are responsible for repairs for damages caused by _____

_____

F. When a person is injured on leased property, the person responsible is _____

_____

23-6 Dispossess Actions

Three methods available to landlords to regain possession of the property are

A. _____ B. _____ C. _____

Legal Concepts

For each statement, write T *in the answer column if the statement is true or* F *if the statement is false.*

Answer

1. There must be either an express or implied contract between the parties in the landlord-tenant relationship.

  1. _____

2. The payment of rent by a tenant is essential to the creation of the landlord-tenant relationship.

  2. _____

3. A lodger has the right to bring suit for trespass or to eject an intruder from the premises.

  3. _____

4. A lease confers upon a tenant exclusive possession of the premises as against all the world.

  4. _____

5. The granting of permission to hold a dance party in a hall is considered to be a lease of the hall.

  5. _____

6. In most states a tenancy at will must be evidenced by a writing to satisfy the Statute of Frauds.

  6. _____

7. A periodic tenancy ceases automatically upon the death of the tenant.

  7. _____

8. A lease must contain a definite agreement as to the extent and bounds of the leased property.

  8. _____

9. Many states now have laws, designed to protect tenants, that govern security deposits.

  9. _____

10. A landlord may not discriminate in selecting tenants on the grounds of race, creed, color, or sex.

  10. _____

11. The warranty of habitability applies only to multiple-family dwellings.

  11. _____

12. A landlord can never be prosecuted as a trespasser on his or her own rented property.

  12. _____

13. A landlord has the right to evict a tenant for nonpayment of rent, disorderliness, or illegal use of the premises.

  13. _____

14. Unlawful detainer is a legal procedure that provides a tenant with a quick method for getting action against a landlord.

  14. _____

15. Tenants may be held responsible for injuries to persons caused by defects in areas under the tenants' control.

  15. _____

Name _____ Date _____

Language of the Law

Select the legal term that best matches each definition.

a. actual eviction   f. landlord   k. periodic tenancy
b. assignee   g. lease   l. quiet enjoyment
c. assignor   h. leasehold estate   m. tenancy at sufferance
d. constructive eviction   i. lessee   n. tenancy at will
e. ejectment   j. lessor   o. tenancy for years

Answer

1. The common-law name for the lawsuit brought by a landlord to have a tenant evicted from the premises
2. The situation that arises when a tenant is physically deprived of a leasehood
3. Another name for the landlord who gives the lease to a tenant
4. The right of a tenant to the undisturbed possession of the property leased
5. A tenancy that continues for successive periods until one of the parties terminates it by giving notice to the other party
6. The agreement that gives rise to the landlord-tenant relationship
7. An estate for a definite or fixed period of time
8. Another name for a tenant
9. The type of tenancy that arises when a tenant wrongfully remains in possession of the premises after expiration of the tenancy
10. The situation that arises when a tenant is deprived of something that is of a substantial nature that was called for under the lease

1. _____
2. _____
3. _____
4. _____

5. _____
6. _____
7. _____
8. _____

9. _____

10. _____

Applying the Law

1. Ying rented an apartment at the Bay View apartment building. During the winter, the owner of the building failed to remove the snow and ice from the steps leading to the main entrance of the building. A friend of Ying's slipped on the steps and injured her back. Was Ying responsible for the injuries? Why or why not.

_____
_____

2. While visiting Rice's apartment, Burke slipped on a loose scatter rug and broke her arm. Rice had placed the small scatter rug on a newly polished floor. Burke sued the owner of the apartment building for negligence. Would she win the case? Explain.

_____
_____

3. On October 15, Wright rented an apartment at the Superior Apartments building for a period of one year. After living there for a month, Wright discovered that the furnace was broken and that the apartment had no heat. Wright notified the landlord, but nothing was done to repair the furnace. When the temperature dropped to 38 degrees, Wright moved out. The owner of the building sued Wright for the balance of the rent due for the year. Did Wright win the case? Why or why not?

_____
_____
_____

4. Rogers rented a cottage on Marilee Lake for one year under a periodic tenancy. One month after entering into the tenancy, Rogers died. Shortly thereafter, Rogers's daughter, Shirley, moved into the cottage. The landlord brought suit to evict Shirley on the grounds that Rogers's death ended the tenancy. Did Shirley win the case? Explain.

_____

_____

5. Denver Realty rented a house to Garcia under a periodic tenancy. Terms of the lease required her to inform the landlord 90 days prior to the end of the lease of her intention of terminating the leasehold. Garcia neglected to do so, moving to an apartment one weekend without warning and then failing to make lease payments to Denver. Did the lease come to an end when Garcia moved out? Why or why not?

_____

_____

6. Electra Arms rented Hambright an apartment for one year, requiring a security deposit of $700. The apartment manager refused to return Hambright's deposit at the end of the leasehold, claiming that the $700 would be used in preparing the apartment for the next tenant. Hambright left no damage or excessive-use depreciation when he vacated the apartment. Did Electra Arms have the right to retain Hambright's $700? Explain.

_____

_____

7. Vargas's rented house was entered by the landlord during Vargas's absence and without his permission. The landlord customarily made periodic visits to rented properties to observe their condition. Vargas charged the landlord with trespassing. The lease contained no condition relating to landlord inspection. Was the landlord a trespasser? Why or why not?

_____

_____

8. While attending college away from home, Soroka boarded with a private family. She had her own room and received two meals each day. Was she considered to be a tenant? Explain.

_____

_____

9. Basinger's one-year lease expired, but she refused to leave her apartment even though she was requested to by her landlord and was given proper notice. Her tender of rent for the first month of the next year was refused. She claimed that she was a tenant at will. Was she correct? Why or why not?

_____

_____

10. O'Brian rented a house from the American Fruit Farms Company during his employment as a seasonal worker with the company. After two months, his employment with the company was terminated, and the American Fruit Farms Company requested him to move out of the house immediately. O'Brian did not comply with the request, and the company sought to have him removed by court order. Would the court allow O'Brian to stay longer? Explain.

_____

_____

24 Wills, Intestacy, and Trusts

Chapter Outline

24-1 Testamentary Disposition of Property

A. When people die with a will, their property goes to _____

_____

B. When people die without a will, their property goes to _____

_____

24-2 Testacy

A. A will may be made by _____

B. In determining sound mind, the court asks

　　1. _____

　　2. _____

　　3. _____

　　4. _____

C. With the exception of an oral will, a will must be _____

_____

D. A will must be signed by _____

E. With the exception of some handwritten wills, a will must be witnessed by _____

_____

F. In many states, persons and their spouses who witness a will may not _____

_____

G. In some states, witnesses are not required for _____

_____

H. In some states, oral wills may be made by _____

I. Among the devices to protect surviving family members when a spouse dies are

　　1. _____

　　2. _____

　　3. _____

J. A surviving spouse who does not like the provisions of a deceased spouse's will may

_____

K. Children left out of a will are protected if they can prove _____

_____

L. Adopted children are given _____

_____

M. A will may be revoked by

1. _____

2. _____

3. _____

N. A will may be contested on the grounds of

1. _____

2. _____

3. _____

24-3 Intestacy   Under a typical statute, if a person dies intestate,

A. The rights of a surviving spouse are

1. _____

2. _____

3. _____

B. The rights of other heirs are

1. _____

2. _____

3. _____

4. _____

5. _____

24-4 Settling an Estate When people die owning assets, their estates must be _____

_____

24-5 Trusts   **A.** In trust, title is split between _____

B. A testamentary trust is _____

C. A living trust comes into existence _____

D. The trustee is obligated by law to _____

Legal Concepts

For each statement, write T *in the answer column if the statement is true* or F *if the statement is false.*

Answer

1. The issue of soundness of mind of a person who makes a will is always raised when someone dies.

1. _____

2. A person of any age may make a will.

2. _____

3. Undue influence is a valid reason for a will to be declared invalid.

3. _____

4. The laws governing the making and signing of wills are uniform throughout the United States.

4. _____

5. A will must be signed by the testator, unless the testator is physically unable to do so.

5. _____

6. When a person dies intestate, both real and personal property are distributed according to the laws of the state where the deceased was domiciled.

6. _____

7. A parent may not disinherit a child.

7. *F*

8. Adopted children are given the same legal rights as natural children.

8. _____

9. Surviving spouses are not assured a share of their spouse's estate.

9. *F*

10. A codicil must be executed with the same formalities as a will.

10. _____

11. In a declaration of trust, the settlor holds the legal title to the property as trustee for the benefit of some other person.

11. _____

12. The chief objection to a spray trust is that it gives the trustee too much control.
13. Property placed in trust may be preserved for beneficiaries for 100 years or more.
14. A living trust is a trust that is created by a will.
15. The income from an irrevocable trust is not taxable to the settlor.

12. _____
13. _____
14. _____
15. _____

Language of the Law

Select the legal term that best matches each definition.

a. administrator
b. beneficiary
c. bequest
d. codicil
e. devise

f. executor
g. heir
h. holographic will
i. *inter vivos* trust
j. intestate

k. nuncupative will
l. probate
m. settlor
n. surety
o. testamentary trust

Answer

1. The procedure whereby an estate is managed and closed under the supervision of a court
2. A person appointed to take charge of an estate when the deceased has left no will
3. A term given to the estate of someone who dies without having prepared a valid will
4. A supplement to a will
5. A will written entirely in the handwriting of the testator
6. Real property that is left by a will
7. The person who establishes a trust
8. One who received property by a will
9. Another name for a living trust
10. A person or insurance company that stands behind the executor

1. ___L_____
2. ___A_____
3. ___J_____
4. ___D_____
5. ___H_____
6. ___E_____
7. ___m_____
8. ___B_____
9. ___I_____
10. ___N_____

Applying the Law

1. Vickers, angry at his wife, made a will leaving his entire estate to charity. Vickers specifically wrote in the will that he intended to leave his wife nothing. Would Vickers' wishes be carried out? Explain.

_____
_____
_____

2. Haley, a 16-year-old singing sensation known throughout the United States, made a will leaving his large estate to his sister, Kathleen. Haley was killed in an automobile accident. For what legal reason did Haley's parents inherit his estate rather than Kathleen?

_____
_____
_____

3. Pierce's will left her estate in equal shares to a natural daughter, an adopted daughter, and two stepsons. The daughters claimed that the stepsons could not legally inherit from Pierce. Were the daughters correct? Why or why not?

_____
_____
_____
_____

4. Singleton, an 80-year-old widower, made a will leaving everything to his son, Jason. A year later, Singleton remarried and died a week after that. Would Jason inherit his father's entire estate? Explain.

_____

_____

_____

5. Thurber prepared a will without the assistance of an attorney. With all intent to leave his estate to his children, Thurber wrote, "I leave my real and personal property to my heirs." Why might Thurber's children not inherit the entire estate?

_____

_____

_____

6. A short time before her death, Holsinger decided to remove the name of a former friend from among those to benefit from her estate. Holsinger blanked out the name and inserted another name in its place. Would the person whose name was newly inserted in the will inherit from Holsinger's estate? Why or why not?

_____

_____

_____

7. Handy signed a will at the office of a bank. The bank president took the will to his office and had it witnessed by secretaries working in the office. Handy was not present at the time. In the event of a dispute after Handy's death, would the will be allowed? Explain.

_____

_____

_____

8. Longfellow, when 80 years old, prepared a new will. In writing the will, the testator distributed the estate among six of his seven children. After Longfellow's death, the unmentioned child claimed equal rights with the others who were named as beneficiaries. For what legal reason could the seventh child inherit?

_____

_____

_____

9. Thornton lived alone, was very ill, and had no one to care for her. She was wealthy, but would not go to an attorney or engage a nurse because of her frugality. Thornton wrote a will in her own handwriting, signed her name, Elizabeth Thornton, and placed it among other papers in her family Bible. Why could this will be probated in certain states?

_____

_____

_____

10. Selby was a successful inventor with many inventions and patents to his credit. He was self-trained, had never gone to school, and could neither read nor write. At an advanced age, he had an attorney prepare a will, which was signed with an X and witnessed by younger associates of the inventor. Would such a signature satisfy the demands of probate? Why or why not?

_____

_____

_____

25 Nature and Kinds of Commercial Paper

Chapter Outline

25-1 Purpose of Commercial Paper

The purpose of commercial paper is to _____
_____
_____

25-2 Concept of Negotiability

When an instrument is transferred by negotiation, _____
_____

25-3 Kinds of Negotiable Instruments

There are three basic kinds of negotiable instruments

A. A draft is _____

   1. A sight draft is _____

   2. A time draft is _____

   3. A trade acceptance is _____

   4. A check is _____

B. A note is _____

   1. A demand note is _____

   2. A time note is _____

   3. An installment note is _____

C. A certificate of deposit is _____
_____

25-4 Parties to Commercial Paper

In addition to drawers of drafts and checks, makers of notes, and payees of both types of instruments, other parties to commercial paper are the following:

A. A bearer is _____
_____

B. A holder is _____
_____

C. A holder in due course is _____
_____

D. An indorser is _____
_____

E. An indorsee is _____
_____

F. An acceptor is _____

25-5 Requirements of Negotiability

To be negotiable, an instrument must be

A. _____

B. _____

25-6 Dates and
Controlling
Words

A. The omission of the date _____

B. Words control _____

Legal Concepts

For each statement, write T *in the answer column if the statement is true or* F *if the statement is false.*

Answer

1. The concept of negotiability is one of the most important features of commercial paper.
2. When an instrument is transferred by negotiation, the transferee may receive greater rights than the transferor had.
3. The person who is requested to pay the money in a draft is called the payee.
4. A draft payable "30 days after sight" is an example of a sight draft.
5. A trade acceptance is a draft that is often used in combination with a bill of lading.
6. A check is the most common type of draft.
7. Notes are order instruments involving three persons.
8. A negotiable instrument written in pencil would be considered to be a negligent writing.
9. An instrument that is conditional is not negotiable.
10. A writing that says "IOU $500" is negotiable.
11. An acceleration clause is another name for an extension clause.
12. The omission of the date affects the negotiability of an instrument.
13. An instrument may be predated or postdated without having its negotiability affected.
14. The failure to number an instrument affects its negotiability.
15. An instrument may be payable to the order of an estate, trust, or fund.

1. _T_
2. ____
3. _F_
4. ____
5. ____
6. _T_
7. ____
8. ____
9. ____
10. _F_
11. ____
12. ____
13. ____
14. ____
15. ____

Language of the Law

Select the legal term that best matches each definition.

a. acceptor
b. bearer
c. certificate of deposit
d. check
e. demand note

f. draft
g. drawee
h. drawer
i. holder
j. indorser

k. installment note
l. maker
m. payee
n. sight draft
o. time draft

Answer

1. The person to whom a negotiable instrument is made payable
2. A drawee of a draft who has promised to honor the draft as presented by signing it on its face
3. An order instrument through which the person writing it orders another person to pay money to a third person
4. A written order on the drawee to pay on demand the amount named in the instrument
5. The person on whom a draft or check is drawn
6. The person in physical possession of a commercial paper indorsed in blank or payable to bearer
7. The person who creates a draft or check by writing it
8. The person who makes and signs a promise instrument such as a promissory note

1. _M_
2. _A_
3. _F_
4. _N_
5. _G_
6. _B_
7. _H_
8. _L_

9. An ordinary note in which the principal is payable in a series of payments at specified times

10. A draft drawn on a bank and payable on demand

9. _K_____

10. _P_____

Applying the Law

1. An envelope containing a ten-dollar rebate check was placed in Wilson's mailbox by mistake. It was addressed to Tarbox, a former tenant of the apartment, and read, "Pay to the bearer or J. Tarbox, $10.00." Was Wilson a holder of the check? Why or why not?

_____

_____

2. While browsing through Kinkaid's antique shop in Georgetown, Massachusetts, a tourist from Mexico found a chair that he wanted to buy. The price was $600. Since the tourist was short of money, Kinkaid agreed to take $400 in cash and the balance in a promissory note. The tourist made the note payable to the order of Kinkaid in the amount of 458,000 Mexican pesos. Later, Kinkaid showed the note to a friend, who said that it was not negotiable. Was the friend correct? Explain.

_____

_____

3. The next day, the same tourist returned to Kinkaid's antique shop to ask a question about the chair he had purchased. Kinkaid gave back the note that the tourist had given him the day before in exchange for a note payable to his order in the amount of "$200 worth of silver." Was the new note negotiable? Why or why not?

_____

_____

4. Sukys, a noted author, received a royalty check from his publisher, which read, "Pay to Paul Sukys the sum of $4,500." Was the check negotiable? Why or why not?

_____

_____

5. Streeter gave her daughter the following instrument: "September 1, 19—, Due Jeanne Streeter $1,000, when she is 18 years old. [Signed] Edna Streeter." Jeanne Streeter, the payee, attempted to negotiate the instrument to a bank. The bank refused to take it, saying that it was not negotiable. Was the bank correct? Explain.

_____

_____

6. "October 17, 19—, Winchester, Massachusetts. Eighteen months after date, I promise to pay to the order of Margaret Otis, $1,000 with interest. Given in payment of merchandise. [Signed] Henry Mohr." Is this instrument negotiable? Why or why not?

_____

_____

7. "December 5, 19—, Albuquerque, New Mexico. Two years after date, pay to the order of Xavier Monaco, $500 with interest. [Signed] Monte Miranda. To: Leon Sloboda, 29 Caballo Avenue, Las Cruces, New Mexico." Is this instrument a draft? Explain.

_____

_____

_____

8. "March 7, 19—, Tucson, Arizona. Six months after date, pay to the order of Evert Lighthill, $300 with interest. Given in payment of a moped. [Signed] Dominick Rosa. To: Janet Turpin Jalea de Catalan, Veracruz, Mexico." Is this a domestic bill of exchange? Why or why not?

_____

_____

_____

9. Harper received a time draft, drawn on him by the Wilmington Department Store. He filed it with other papers and did not return it to Wilmington. Harper later denied any responsibility on the draft, claiming that he had not accepted it for payment. An action for its payment was brought by the Wilmington Department Store. Was Harper liable on the draft? Why or why not?

_____

_____

_____

10. Vanech, a landscape contractor, received a $400 check for work done. The check was postdated one week because the person for whom Vanech did the work did not have enough money in the bank at the time to cover it. Was the check negotiable? Explain.

_____

_____

_____

26 Negotiation of Commercial Paper

Chapter Outline

26-1 Assignment Versus Negotiation

A. Commercial paper is assigned when _____
_____

B. Negotiation is the transfer _____
_____

   1. To be negotiated, order paper must be _____

   2. Bearer paper may be negotiated by _____
_____

26-2 Negotiation by Indorsement

A. Under Regulation CC, _____
_____

B. A blank indorsement consists of _____
_____

C. A special indorsement is made by _____
_____

D. A restrictive indorsement limits the _____
_____

E. A qualified indorsement is one in which _____
_____

26-3 Significance of Indorsements

A. An indorser who receives consideration for an instrument warrants that

   1. _____

   2. _____

   3. _____

   4. _____

   5. _____

B. Unless an indorsement states otherwise, every indorser agrees _____
_____

C. An accommodation party is _____

26-4 Multiple Payees and Missing Indorsements

A. If an instrument is payable to either of two payees, _____
_____

B. If an instrument is payable to both of two payees, _____
_____

C. A depository bank may supply _____
_____

26-5 Forged or Unauthorized Indorsements

A. With three exceptions and, unless ratified, an unauthorized or forged signature

_____

B. The exceptions are

1. _____

2. _____

3. _____

Legal Concepts

For each statement, write T *in the answer column if the statement is true or* F *if the statement is false.*

Answer

1. People who receive instruments by assignment are given the same special protection given to those who receive instruments by negotiation.

    1. _____

2. An assignment of commercial paper occurs by operation of law when the holder of an instrument dies.

    2. _____

3. If an instrument is payable to "bearer" or to "cash," it is called order paper.

    3. F_____

4. Indorsements may be written in ink, typed, or rubber-stamped.

    4. _____

5. The Uniform Commercial Code (UCC) requires that indorsements be placed on the back of instruments.

    5. _____

6. An instrument that is indorsed with a special indorsement must be indorsed by the indorsee before it can be further negotiated.

    6. _____

7. A conditional indorsement makes the rights of the indorsee subject to the happening of a certain event.

    7. _____

8. A qualified indorser accepts liability for payment of an instrument.

    8. _____

9. An indorser warrants that all signatures are genuine or authorized.

    9. _____

10. An accommodation party is not liable to the party accommodated.

    10. _____

11. An indorser warrants that no defense of any party is good against him or her.

    11. _____

12. When an instrument is dishonored, indorsers have no obligation where proper presentment has been made and notice of dishonor has been given to them.

    12. _____

13. There are no exceptions to the general rule that an unauthorized indorsement has no effect.

    13. _____

14. An instrument payable to two payees in the alternative, for example, "Pay to the order of B. Bell *or* R. Alt," requires the indorsement of both payees to be negotiated.

    14. _____

15. The burden of preventing padded payrolls is on the drawer of payroll checks.

    15. _____

Language of the Law

Select the legal term that best matches each definition.

a. accommodation party
b. *allonge*
c. assignment
d. bearer paper
e. blank indorsement

f. conditional indorsement
g. dishonored
h. indorsee
i. indorsement
j. negotiation

k. order paper
l. qualified indorsement
m. restrictive indorsement
n. special indorsement
o. without recourse

Answer

1. Another name for a full indorsement

    1. _____

2. An indorsement in which no particular indorsee is specified

    2. _____

3. The transfer of a contract right from one person to another

    3. _____

4. Not paid by the maker or drawee

    4. G_____

5. The transfer of an instrument in such form that the transferee becomes a holder

    5. _____

6. An indorsement in which the words *without recourse* are used

    6. _____

7. Another name for a rider attached to a negotiable instrument

7. _____

8. A person who signs an instrument in any capacity for the purpose of lending his or her name to another party to the instrument

8. _____

9. An instrument that is payable to "bearer" or "cash"

9. _____

10. An indorsement that makes the rights of the indorsee subject to the happening of a certain event or condition

10. _____

Applying the Law

1. Letvin placed her paycheck on her desk and went for a cup of coffee. The check was payable to her order in the amount of $480. She had not indorsed it. When Letvin returned, she discovered that the check was missing. Later the check was found in the possession of Henderson, a fellow employee who had taken it from Letvin's desk without authority. Was the transfer of the check to Henderson's possession a negotiation? Explain.

_____

_____

2. When Fielding received his paycheck, he indorsed it in blank, placed it on his desk, and went to get a cup of coffee. The check accidentally blew out an open window. Curren, a stranger to Fielding, found the check on the sidewalk below, took it to a bank, and cashed it. Was the transfer of the check to the bank a negotiation? Why or why not?

_____

_____

3. When Hernandez received her paycheck, she indorsed it with a restrictive indorsement, placed it in an envelope with a deposit slip, and mailed it to the bank for deposit to her account. Why was the restrictive indorsement a good one to use for this transaction?

_____

_____

4. Coughlin was an indorser on a check. A subsequent holder presented the check to the bank named on the instrument and was informed that the drawer did not have an account at the bank. Coughlin, as an indorser, was called upon for payment of the check. Must Coughlin pay the subsequent holder of the instrument? Explain.

_____

_____

5. LeVander forged the signature of Gore to a note which she negotiated to Burns for value. Burns then indorsed and delivered the note to Gossett as a down payment on a used car. When Gossett presented the note to Gore for payment, the forgery was recognized. Gossett demanded payment from Burns. Burns claimed innocence of any knowledge of the forgery and therefore freedom from liability. Would a court rule for Gossett in an action against Burns? Why or why not?

_____

_____

_____

_____

6. Raughley indorsed a check as follows: "John R. Raughley, without recourse." The check was subsequently found to have been raised from $90 to $900. A later holder claimed that Raughley was liable on the instrument, since it was not honored by the bank because of the alteration. Raughley denied liability on the basis of the qualified indorsement he had used. Did the qualified indorsement allow Raughley to avoid liability for payment of the check? Explain.

_____

_____

7. Bigelow received a check from her insurance company in settlement of a claim. The words *Payee's indorsement required* were printed on the back of the check. Bigelow mailed the check together with two other checks to the bank for deposit in her account without indorsing them. Could the check from the insurance company be deposited in Bigelow's account without her indorsement? Why or why not?

_____

_____

8. Burton borrowed $1,000 from Roberts and in return signed a promissory note payable in one year with interest at 12 percent. Roberts later negotiated the note to Green, who was a friend of Burton. When it became due, Green agreed to extend the time of the note for an additional three months, on the promise from Burton that the 12 percent interest would be paid during the extended period of time. At the end of the three months, Burton dishonored the note, claiming insufficient funds. Green proceeded to sue Roberts, the indorser. Was Roberts liable on the note? Why or why not?

_____

_____

9. Jewell, Jennings, and Jaworoski were indorsers on a draft that had been accepted by Schwartz. When the draft was presented for payment, Schwartz claimed insolvency and refused to pay it. The holder took no action for three weeks, hoping that Schwartz's financial condition would improve. When payment was not forthcoming, the holder finally decided to notify Jewell, Jennings, and Jaworoski that they were being held responsible on the dishonored draft. They refused to pay, claiming the presentment and notice of dishonor were unnecessarily delayed beyond the time such presentment and notice are due. Were they liable on the draft? Explain.

_____

_____

10. Wong agreed to indorse a personal check for a visiting business associate when he learned that the local bank with whom he had an account would not cash it because of the person's out-of-state address and credit references. The check was returned for lack of sufficient funds, and the bank charged Wong's account for the amount. Wong claimed that he was not liable on the check because he had received no consideration for his indorsement. Was Wong correct? Explain.

_____

_____

27 Holders in Due Course, Defenses, and Liabilities

Chapter Outline

27-1 Holder in Due Course

A. A holder in due course is _____

_____

B. A holder is someone who is in possession of an instrument that is _____

_____

C. People give value for an instrument when _____

_____

D. Good faith means _____

E. A holder has notice that an instrument is overdue when _____

_____

F. A holder who receives an instrument from a holder in due course acquires _____

_____

27-2 Personal Defenses

A. Personal defenses are defenses that cannot be used against _____

B. The most common personal defenses are

1. _____

2. _____

3. _____

4. _____

5. _____

6. _____

27-3 Real Defenses

A. Real defenses can be used against _____

B. The following are real defenses

1. _____

2. _____

3. _____

4. _____

5. _____

6. _____

27-4 Liability of the Parties

A. Primary liability is _____

B. Two parties that have primary liability are

1. _____

2. _____

C. Secondary liability is _____

_____

D. Two types of parties that have secondary liability are

1. _____

2. _____

E. The conditions required to hold a secondary party liable are

1. _____

2. _____

3. _____

Legal Concepts

For each statement, write T *in the answer column if the statement is true or* F *if the statement is false.*

Answer

1. Holders in due course receive more rights than their transferors had.
2. A payee may not be a holder in due course.
3. To be a holder in due course, the holder must take an instrument in good faith.
4. If an instrument is transferred to a person as a gift, that person would not qualify as a holder in due course.
5. People do not give value for instruments when they accept instruments in payment of debts.
6. An individual who is on notice that an instrument is overdue may be a holder in due course.
7. A holder who receives title to an instrument from someone who is a holder in due course receives all the rights of the holder in due course.
8. Personal defenses are defenses that can be used against a holder in due course.
9. Lack of consideration is a defense that may not be used against a holder in due course.
10. The defense of fraud in the inducement may be used against a holder in due course.
11. An instrument that is associated with an illegal act is not collectible by anyone, not even by a holder in due course.
12. No person is liable on an instrument unless his or her signature appears thereon or is written by an authorized agent.
13. The maker of a promissory note has primary liability.
14. Failure of the holder to present a draft for payment, unless excused, discharges the drawer from all obligation on the instrument.
15. Notice of dishonor of an instrument must be given in writing to the drawer and the indorsers.

1. _____
2. _____
3. _____

4. _____

5. _____

6. _____

7. _____
8. _____
9. _____
10. _____

11. _____

12. _____
13. _____

14. _____

15. _____

Language of the Law

Select the legal term that best matches each definition.

a. delivery
b. failure of consideration
c. good faith
d. holder
e. holder in due course

f. lack of consideration
g. limited defense
h. personal defense
i. presentment
j. primary liability

k. protest
l. real defense
m. secondary liability
n. shelter provision
o. universal defense

Answer

1. The liability that occurs when a party promises to pay the instrument without any reservations of any kind
2. A rule allowing a holder who receives an instrument from a holder in due course to receive all the rights of the former party
3. A holder who takes an instrument for value, in good faith, and without notice that it is overdue or has been dishonored

1. _____

2. _____

3. _____

4. A certificate of dishonor that states that a draft was presented for acceptance (or payment) and was dishonored

5. A defense that may be used when no consideration existed in the underlying contract for which the instrument was issued

6. A defense that may not be used against a holder in due course

7. A person who is in possession of a negotiable instrument that is issued or indorsed to that person's order or to bearer

8. The liability that occurs only after certain conditions have been met

9. The transfer of possession from one person to another

10. Another name for a universal defense

4 _____

5. _____

6. _____

7. _____

8. _____

9. _____

10. _____

Applying the Law

1. Malone found a check on the sidewalk that was payable to the order of Kenneth Johnson in the amount of $450. Malone indorsed his own name on the check and cashed it at a bank. Was the bank a holder in due course of the check? Why or why not?

_____

_____

_____

2. Tarrant wrote a check payable to the order of his daughter, Jessica, in the amount of $100 and gave it to her as a birthday gift. Was Jessica a holder in due course of the instrument? Why or why not?

_____

_____

3. Jessica Tarrant indorsed the $100 check that she had received as a gift from her father with a special indorsement and gave it to Watson in payment for a used TV set. Watson indorsed the check in blank and gave it to his son, Tom, as a gift. Did Tom have the rights of a holder in due course? Explain.

_____

_____

_____

4. Crenshaw bought a tool set from National Supply Co. and signed a consumer credit contract agreeing to pay the amount of $798.00 in 12 monthly installments. National Supply Co. had an arrangement with Ace Finance Company to finance National's customers' purchases and immediately negotiated the credit contract to Ace in exchange for payment. The tool set turned out to be defective. Could Crenshaw use the defense of a defective tool set (a personal defense) if he is sued by Ace Finance Company for the money owed? Why or why not?

_____

_____

_____

5. VonKlatz, a minor, purchased a used Mercedes-Benz from Foreign Car Service, Inc. In payment, she gave $2,000 in cash and a promissory note for the balance of $10,000 to be paid with interest at, or after, 120 days. The dealer discounted the note at the bank. When the bank presented the note for payment, VonKlatz refused to pay it. Did she have a real defense against the bank's demand for payment? Why or why not?

_____

_____

_____

_____

6. Creedon was employed as a maintenance worker by Weaver Realty Co. While cleaning an office, Creedon found a paper on which an officer of Weaver Realty had written her signature. Creedon executed a note payable 30 days after sight above the signature and negotiated the instrument by indorsement to an acquaintance for value. When the note was presented for payment, the Weaver Realty officer refused to pay. Did the holder have rights against the alleged maker of the note? Explain.

_____

_____

7. Moynihan executed and left on her desk a promissory note made out to Pappas. Moynihan owed Pappas the money specified on the note for her purchase of a lawn tractor a week previously. Pappas was admitted to Moynihan's office, saw the note made out to her, picked it up, and departed without seeing Moynihan. Pappas negotiated the note to her bank through indorsement and delivery. When the bank presented the note for payment, Moynihan refused, claiming she had not delivered the note to the indorser. Did Moynihan have a defense against the bank? Why or why not?

_____

_____

8. Lathrop employed Croydon as agent to purchase a tract of commercially zoned land for him. He gave Croydon $1,000 in cash and a draft for $3,000 made payable to the order of Croydon with instructions that the cash and draft be used as a down payment on the property. Croydon indorsed and delivered the draft to Jablonsky, a holder in due course. Jablonsky sued when Lathrop refused payment on the draft. Lathrop's defense was that Croydon had betrayed his trust by not using the draft as directed. Could Jablonsky require Lathrop to honor the draft? Explain.

_____

_____

9. Washington accepted for value, by indorsement from a holder in due course, a check that had been altered from an original amount of $75 to $750. After investigation, it was learned that the drawer of the check had not taken the usual and ordinary precautions in drawing the check, thus making the alteration possible. The drawer contended that he was not liable for the $750, but only for the original amount, $75, for which the check was drawn. Was the drawer's contention correct? Why or why not?

_____

_____

10. McDougal executed and delivered a 90-day note for $3,000 payable to bearer and dated August 22,19—. Someone erased the date and wrote in ink the words "December 19, 19—" over the erasure. The alteration was obvious to anyone who examined the note. Why can't someone who purchases the note after the alteration be a holder in due course?

_____

_____

28 Checks and Bank Collections

Chapter Outline

28-1 Checks

A. A check is _____

B. Any writing, no matter how crude, may be _____

_____

C. Special checks include the following

    1. A bank draft is _____

_____

    2. A cashier's check is _____

_____

    3. Traveler's checks are _____

_____

D. "Certification of a check is acceptance" means _____

_____

E. A check may be postdated when _____

_____

28-2 Electronic Fund Transfers (EFTs)

When an automatic teller machine (ATM) card is stolen, a consumer's liability is limited

to _____

28-3 Bank Deposits and Collections

A. Terms to describe banks are as follows

    1. Depositary bank means _____

    2. Payor bank means _____

    3. Intermediary bank means _____

    4. Collecting bank means _____

    5. Presenting bank means _____

    6. Remitting bank means _____

B. The life cycle of a check begins _____

_____

28-4 The Bank-Depositor Relationship

A. The drawee bank is under a duty to honor _____

_____

B. The bank is under no obligation to a customer to pay a _____

C. After the death of the drawer, a bank may pay or certify checks for _____

_____

D. If a bank, in good faith, pays an altered amount to a holder, it may deduct from the drawer's account only _____

E. Funds from checks drawn on

    1. a bank draft must be made available _____

    _____

    2. banks within the same Federal Reserve district must be made available _____

    _____

    3. banks outside the bank's Federal Reserve district must be made available _____

    _____

F. Payor banks are required to either settle or return checks _____

G. Depositors owe a duty to banks in which they have checking accounts to _____

    _____

H. Most states have statutes making it larceny or attempted larceny for _____

    _____

I. The UCC imposes a duty on depositors to _____

    _____

J. Stop-payment orders are binding on the bank

    1. if oral for _____

    2. if in writing for _____   _____

Legal Concepts

For each statement, write T *in the answer column if the statement is true or* F *if the statement is false.*

Answer

1. A check is the most common form of a note.   1. *F* _____
2. A bank must honor a check when the check is properly drawn against a credit balance of the drawer.   2. _____
3. The use of a printed form to write a check is required.   3. _____
4. When the buyer is unknown to the seller, personal checks are more acceptable than bank drafts.   4. _____
5. The UCC places no obligation on a bank to certify a check if it does not wish to do so.   5. _____
6. Postdating a check has the effect of turning a demand instrument into a time instrument.   6. *T* _____
7. Under the Electronic Fund Transfer Act, consumers are entitled to either receive a written receipt at the time of the transaction or to have the transaction appear on the periodic statement sent to the consumer.   7. _____
8. If a consumer notifies the issuer of the loss or theft of an ATM card within four business days, the consumer is liable for only $50 of any unauthorized withdrawals made with the card.   8. _____
9. The unauthorized use of an ATM card is a criminal offense.   9. _____
10. Any settlement given by a depositary bank on a check is provisional.   10. _____
11. Banks must discontinue honoring checks of a deceased person within three days after the person's death.   11. _____
12. The bank is liable to a depositor if it gives payment for any check to which the depositor's signature has been forged.   12. _____
13. Banks must either pay or return checks on or before their midnight deadline.   13. *T* _____
14. Depositors have only three months to notify the bank of a forged indorsement on a check.   14. *F* _____
15. A written stop-payment order is binding for 14 days.   15. _____

110

Language of the Law

Select the legal term that best matches each definition.

a. bank draft   f. depositary bank   k. presenting bank
b. cashier's check   g. forgery   l. stale check
c. certified check   h. intermediary bank   m. subrogation
d. check   i. overdraft   n. traveler's check
e. collecting bank   j. payor bank   o. uttering

Answer

1. The situation that occurs when the bank pays out more money than the customer has on deposit
2. The first bank to which an item is transferred for collection, even though it is also the payor bank
3. A draft drawn on a bank and payable on demand
4. The act of fraudulently making or altering a check or other form of commercial paper to the injury of another
5. The right of a bank to substitute itself for another party
6. The offering of a forged instrument to another person, when the offeror knows the instrument has been forged
7. A check that has been presented for payment more than six months after the date it was made out
8. A check drawn by a bank upon itself, called an official check
9. A check drawn by one bank on another bank in which it has funds on deposit in favor of a third party
10. A check for which the issuing financial institution is both the drawer and the drawee and that the purchaser signs when purchased and again when cashed

1. _I_
2. _F_
3. _D_
4. _G_
5. _m_
6. _O_
7. _L_
8. _B_
9. _A_
10. _N_

Applying the Law

1. Brown removed a check from his uncle's checkbook, wrote out a check for $200, and forged his uncle's signature on the signature line. He then told his sister what he had done and asked his sister to cash the check for him. Brown's sister went to the bank and attempted to cash the check, but the forgery was detected by an alert teller. Could Brown's sister be charged with a crime? Why or why not?

_____
_____
_____

2. A thief stole Barkley's ATM card, learned her identification number, and withdrew $600 from her bank account without authority. Barkley notified the bank of the theft two days after the card was stolen. Was Barkley's liability limited in this case? Explain.

_____
_____
_____

3. Smith wrote out several checks in payment of his monthly bills. He walked to the post office, mailed the checks, and, on the way home, was struck and killed by a speeding motorist. Since Smith was well-known in the community, the officers of the local bank knew of his death. Was the bank legally able to honor Smith's checks, which arrived a week after he died? Why or why not?

_____
_____
_____

4. O'Connor, who had $6,000 in her bank account at the Second State Bank, wrote a check to the order of Walsh Furniture Co., Inc., in the amount of $4,998. Walsh attempted to cash the check at the Second State Bank, but the bank refused to cash it under the mistaken belief that O'Connor had insufficient funds in the bank. Could Walsh sue the bank for refusing to honor the check? Explain.

_____

_____

_____

5. Suppose that, in the above case, O'Connor had made the check out to Walsh Furniture Co. in payment for a set of furniture that was on sale for only three days, and the regular price of the furniture was $1,000 greater than the sale price. Suppose, also, that because of the failure of the bank to honor the check, Walsh Furniture Co. refused to sell the furniture to O'Connor at the sale price. Would the bank be responsible to O'Connor for the loss? Why or why not?

_____

_____

_____

6. Adams, in reconciling her bank statement, discovered among her canceled checks a check that she had not written out. Upon careful examination it was found to be a clever forgery. Because Adams's genuine signature and the forged signature were very similar, the bank had not recognized the forgery. Was the bank liable to Adams for the amount of the forged check? Why or why not?

_____

_____

_____

7. Carlson gave his personal check in payment of his electric bill. The check was returned to the utility company by the bank marked "insufficient funds." Carlson made no effort to pay the check when requested to do so by the payee. What crime, if any, did Carlson commit?

_____

_____

_____

8. Popovic telephoned her bank requesting that it stop payment on a $97.50 check she had written that day in payment for a microwave oven that turned out to be defective. Three weeks later, the check was presented to the bank for collection. The bank paid it and deducted $97.50 from Popovic's account. Did Popovic have legal recourse against the bank? Why or why not?

_____

_____

_____

9. Coady drew a check in favor of Tinti in payment of a bill and postdated the check to a date three weeks later. Tinti claimed that the check was not negotiable. Was Tinti correct? Explain.

_____

_____

_____

10. Noonan wrote out a check to Manreps. Manreps received the check, put it in her bureau drawer, and forgot about it. She came upon the check months later and attempted to cash it at the drawee bank. That bank refused to pay it, claiming that it could not do so by law because the check was so old. Was the bank correct? Why or why not?

_____

_____

_____

29 The Nature of the Insurance Contract

Chapter Outline

A. Insurance is _____

B. The parties to an insurance contract include

    1. _____

    2. _____

    3. _____

A. Insurable interest is _____

B. The four most common exemptions from risk in life insurance policies are

    1. _____

    2. _____

    3. _____

    4. _____

C. Three popular optional provisions in life insurance policies are

    1. _____

    2. _____

    3. _____

D. In addition to losses directly attributed to fire, fire insurance will cover claims made for losses from

    1. _____

    2. _____

    3. _____

    4. _____

    5. _____

    6. _____

    7. _____

E. Homeowner's insurance gives protection for _____

F. The most common types of automobile insurance are

    1. _____

    2. _____

    3. _____

    4. _____

    5. _____

    6. _____

7. _____

29-3 Form of the Insurance Contract

A. A binder is _____

_____

B. When the insured stops paying premiums, an insurance contract is said to _____

_____

29-4 Cancellation of Insurance Policies

A. Conditions that permit the cancellation of an insurance policy include

1. _____

2. _____

3. _____

B. Estoppel is _____

_____

Legal Concepts

For each statement, write T *in the answer column if the statement is true or* F *if the statement is false.*

Answer

1. The function of insurance is to distribute each person's risk among all others in a particular group, who may or may not experience loss.

1. _____

2. It is possible to obtain insurance against almost any risk if an individual or business is willing to pay the price.

2. _____

3. A life insurance policy becomes void if the insurable interest terminates.

3. _____

4. Property insurance will remain valid and enforceable even if the insurable interest terminates.

4. _____

5. In most cases, the courts allow a beneficiary to receive benefits under a life insurance policy if the insured is murdered.

5. _____

6. Beneficiaries are never allowed to recover the proceeds of an insurance policy if the insured commits suicide.

6. _____

7. Life insurance policies rarely allow for optional provisions.

7. _____

8. Property insurance can be purchased to protect real and personal property.

8. _____

9. Fire insurance covers only those losses that result directly from fire.

9. _____

10. Liability under automobile collision insurance is limited to the insured's car.

10. _____

11. No-fault insurance provides protection against the risk of being injured by an uninsured motorist.

11. _____

12. Courts will broadly interpret ambiguous terms of an insurance contract in favor of the insured.

12. _____

13. A binder will include all the usual terms that would be included in the actual policy to be issued.

13. _____

14. In many states, by statute, the insurance company has the burden of proof in establishing that a warranty has been broken by the insured.

14. _____

15. To be legally effective, an insurance company's waiver of rights must always be in writing.

15. _____

Language of the Law

Select the legal term that best matches each definition.

a. beneficiary
b. collision insurance
c. comprehensive coverage
d. concealment
e. double indemnity

f. estoppel
g. insurable interest
h. insurance
i. insured
j. insurer

k. misrepresentation
l. policy
m. premium
n. waiver
o. warranty

Answer

1. The contract of insurance
2. A third party who sometimes receives payment of compensation under an insurance contract
3. The financial interest that a policyholder has in the person or property that is insured
4. An accidental death benefit
5. Automobile insurance that provides protection against loss due to fire, lightning, flood, hail, windstorm, riot, vandalism, and theft
6. Consideration paid for insurance
7. A transfer of risk of economic loss from the buyer to the seller, or to the insurance company
8. The party protected by insurance
9. Any intentional withholding of a fact that would be of material importance to the insurance company's decision to issue an insurance contract
10. When the insurance company gives up one of its rights to help the party protected by the insurance

1. _____
2. _____
3. _____
4. _____
5. _____
6. _____
7. _____
8. _____
9. _____
10. _____

Applying the Law

1. Immediately after Susan and Karl Edwards were married, they took out life insurance policies naming one another as beneficiaries. Their marriage ended in divorce after only one year. Nevertheless, they both continued to pay premiums on their policies and never changed beneficiaries. When Susan died three years later, could Karl collect Susan's life insurance? Why or why not?

_____
_____
_____

2. McHenry sold a valuable Picasso original to Prentice. After the purchase, Prentice obtained insurance to cover damage to, or destruction of, the painting. McHenry's insurance policy covering the painting would not expire until six months after the sale. When the painting was destroyed by fire three weeks after the sale, who collected the insurance, McHenry or Prentice? Explain why.

_____
_____
_____

3. Owens took out a life insurance policy naming his business partner, Warner, as beneficiary. He also took out another policy naming his wife as beneficiary. One year later, Owens committed suicide. Warner collected from the insurance company, but Owens's wife did not. Explain why.

_____
_____
_____

4. Lisa and Anthony Darnell took out life insurance policies naming one another as beneficiaries. Each policy was for $100,000. When Lisa was killed in a boating accident, Anthony collected $200,000. Name and explain the optional provision that must have been included in their insurance policies.

_____

_____

_____

5. Neal purchased fire insurance to cover his winter home in Florida. During a tropical storm, Neal's winter home was struck by lightning, which severely damaged the front part of the house; however, no fire resulted. Neal's insurance agent told him that the damage was not covered under the fire insurance policy because no fire resulted. Was the agent correct? Why or why not?

_____

_____

_____

6. While driving on a vacation trip, Rosen lost control of his car. The car ran up on the curb, skidded over Kaplan's front lawn where it destroyed Kaplan's rose bushes, and then smashed into Kaplan's home. What type of auto insurance will Rosen need to cover him for all this property damage? If the insurance company refuses to pay and Kaplan brings suit, what will Kaplan have to prove to win the suit and receive payment for the damage to his property?

_____

_____

_____

7. Wright decided to take out an insurance policy to cover a collection of antique steam engines. On Monday he filled out an application with the Saska Insurance Company. Clifford, an agent for Saska, told Wright it would take until the following Monday for the main office to process the application. Wright was worried about the collection because of a rash of burglaries in his neighborhood. What should Wright and Clifford arrange while waiting for the main office to approve the policy?

_____

_____

8. Graham applied for insurance with the Alexandria Insurance Company for coverage of his hunting lodge. When asked whether any explosives were stored on the property, Graham said there weren't. Actually, he had several sticks of dynamite in a storage chest on the back porch. The lodge was damaged in a windstorm, and the dynamite was discovered. Alexandria refused to pay Graham because of his lie. Will a court uphold this denial? Why or why not?

_____

_____

9. Zanco, an insurance agent for the Conklin Insurance Company, inspected Hyde's home prior to issuing an insurance policy. During the inspection, Zanco discovered that the home was located near a chemical dump. According to his company's specifications, the home was too close to the dump to be considered insurable, but Zanco issued the policy anyway. A month later, Hyde's home was damaged by a chemical fire originating in the dump. Did Conklin have to pay for the damage? Why or why not?

_____

_____

10. Schenk was a test pilot for Dagger Jet Air Production, Inc. After his third crash, Schenk was told by Ross, an insurance agent for Altar State Insurance, that his policy would be canceled unless he agreed to give up his work as a test pilot. Schenk agreed and a new policy was issued that included the new agreement. Schenk continued to fly and was killed in a crash one week later. Could Schenk's beneficiaries collect under the Altar State policy? Why or why not?

_____

_____

116

30 Security Devices

Chapter Outline

30-1 Necessity of Security Devices

A. A security device is _____
_____

B. A secured loan is _____

C. A security interest is _____

D. An unsecured loan is _____
_____

30-2 Real Property as Security

A. A mortgage is _____
_____

B. An origination fee is _____

C. Types of mortgages are

1. _____
2. _____
3. _____
4. _____
5. _____

D. Two federally chartered corporations with publicly traded stock to encourage investment in home mortgages are _____
_____

E. Like a deed, a mortgage must be _____
_____

F. The rights of a mortgagor include

1. _____
2. _____
3. _____
4. _____

G. The duties of a mortgagor include

1. _____
2. _____
3. _____
4. _____

H. The rights of the mortgagee include

1. _____

2. _____

3. _____

4. _____

I. The duties of the mortgagee include

1. _____

2. _____

30-3 Personal Property as Security

A. Collateral is _____

_____

B. A security agreement is _____

C. Attachment is _____

D. A security interest can be perfected in three ways

1. _____

2. _____

3. _____

Legal Concepts

For each statement, write T *in the answer column if the statement is true or* F *if the statement is false.*

Answer

1. Debts are said to be secured when creditors are assured that somehow they will be able to recover their money.   1. _____

2. Most conventional mortgages involve an enormous amount of government backing.   2. _____

3. Variable mortgages need not include a maximum rate.   3. _____

4. The provisions of many deeds of trust allow a trustee to sell a property without going to court.   4. _____

5. If a mortgage is not recorded and a later mortgage is given on the same property, the new mortgage is always superior to the first.   5. _____

6. A failure to record a first mortgage will erase the obligation of the first mortgagor to the first mortgagee.   6. _____

7. The mortgagor has the right to any income produced by the mortgaged property, but cannot assign that right to the mortgagee.   7. _____

8. The mortgagee has the unrestricted right to sell, assign, or transfer the mortgage to a third party.   8. _____

9. Security agreements need not be in writing.   9. _____

10. Creditors may obtain security interests in property acquired by the debtor after the original agreement is entered into.   10. _____

11. When a security interest attaches, it is effective between the debtor, the creditor, and all third parties.   11. _____

12. A purchase money security interest applies only to consumer goods.   12. _____

13. When a financing statement covers such products as crops, timber, minerals, oil, and gas, the statement must contain a description of the real estate associated with the product.   13. _____

14. A perfected security interest prevails over an unperfected security interest.   14. _____

15. After lawfully repossessing goods, the secured party must sell them.   15. _____

Language of the Law

Select the legal term that best matches each definition.

a. acceleration
b. assume the mortgage
c. attachment
d. balloon-payment mortgage
e. deed of trust
f. foreclosure

g. graduated-payment mortgage
h. mortgage
i. perfected
j. purchase money security interest

k. secured loan
l. secured party
m. security agreement
n. security interest
o. subject to the mortgage

Answer

1. A mortgage with monthly payments that increase over the term of the loan   1. _____
2. The mortgagee's right to collect the entire balance due immediately upon the mortgagor's default on one installment payment   2. _____
3. The right of a mortgagee to apply to a court to have property sold when the mortgagor defaults or fails to perform some agreement attached to the mortgage   3. _____
4. The transfer of interest in real property for the purpose of creating a security for a debt   4. _____
5. The right to use collateral to recover a debt   5. _____
6. When a purchaser agrees to buy mortgaged property and to make the mortgage payments   6. _____
7. A security interest that arises when someone lends money to a consumer and then takes a security interest in the goods that the consumer buys   7. _____
8. The legal enforceability of a security interest   8. _____
9. A loan in which the creditor holds something of the debtor's that has value from which the creditor can be paid if the debtor defaults   9. _____
10. A condition that exists when a secured party has done everything that the law requires to give the secured party greater rights to the goods than others have   10. _____

Applying the Law

1. Nolan purchased a pizzeria for $150,000. He had only $20,000 in cash, so he took out a loan for $130,000 from the Fostoria National Bank. When Nolan defaulted on the loan, Fostoria foreclosed and sold the store for $15,293 less than Nolan owed. Nolan believed he no longer owed Fostoria any money. Was Nolan correct? Explain.

_____

2. Erik and Sonja VonLusch purchased a home using a variable-rate mortgage. The rate of interest was tied to the bank's prime interest rate. At the time of the purchase, the rate was 8 percent. The agreement stated that the rate could change annually; however, no maximum rate was ever set. When the VonLusches received notice that their interest rate would jump to 13 percent, they refused to pay the increase, arguing that the original agreement was unenforceable. Were they correct? Why or why not?

_____

3. Durbin purchased a home from Sealy using a deed of trust. The deed of trust was held by the Plymouth American Bank, which acted as trustee. When Durbin defaulted on the payments, Plymouth moved to sell the property without going through a court foreclosure process. Durbin argued that Plymouth must go to court before the property could be sold. Was he correct? Explain.

_____

4. Wallace bought a summer cottage for $35,000. He financed it with a mortgage from Middlesex Building and Loan. Middlesex did not record the mortgage. Lipsky later bought the cottage from Wallace. Lipsky conducted a search and found no mortgage recorded. Once the sale was completed, Wallace argued that he no longer had any rights to the property and, therefore, owed no money to Middlesex. Was he correct? Explain.

5. Ackerman financed the purchase of his beachfront property with a mortgage from the Medina County Farmers Bank. After making only one payment, he failed to make the next four. After repeated attempts to collect the installments plus late fees, Medina accelerated the debt, claiming that Ackerman had to pay the full amount due or face foreclosure. Ackerman argued that Medina had no right to accelerate the loan. Was Ackerman correct? Explain.

6. Hurley purchased a condominium for $89,000, financing the deal with a mortgage from the Dalburg Savings and Loan Association. As part of the deal, Hurley was to pay additional funds into an escrow account for insurance and property taxes. The mortgage installment payment each month was $530. The additional amount for the escrow account was $70. Hurley paid only the $530 each month. After repeated attempts to collect the additional $70 each month, Dalburg accelerated the debt and threatened to foreclose. Hurley argued that the savings and loan could not accelerate the debt because the installment payments were made on time. Was Hurley's argument correct? Explain.

7. Sullivan, Inc., needed to purchase a fiber-optic splicer from Kellerson Electronics. Sullivan made a down payment on the splicer and agreed that Kellerson could repossess the splicer if Sullivan defaulted on any future installment payments. Did Kellerson have a purchase money security interest in the equipment? Why or why not?

8. Goodrich borrowed $1,000 from Vasquez. To secure the loan, Goodrich allowed Vasquez to take possession of his car. Since Vasquez had no garage, he made arrangements to rent space in his neighbor's garage to protect the car. When Goodrich paid off the debt and asked for the car, Vasquez demanded to be reimbursed for the money he'd spent to rent the garage space. Was Vasquez entitled to that reimbursement? Explain.

9. Silvia and Avitto entered into an agreement whereby Avitto borrowed $10,000 from Silvia and Silvia took a security interest in Avitto's next corn and wheat harvest. The financing statement identified Silvia and Avitto by name and included their mailing addresses. Avitto signed the statement, which identified the corn and wheat crops. The county recorder rejected the financing statement. What element did Silvia and Avitto neglect to include?

10. Russell borrowed $7,000 from the Lancaster Financial Network to purchase a motorcycle. Lancaster took a security interest in the cycle and perfected it by filing. Russell made no payments on the loan, so Lancaster sent Banner to repossess the cycle. When Banner arrived at Russell's house, Russell refused to let him near the cycle. Banner told Russell that he had the right to repossess the motorcycle for Lancaster even if he had to use force to do so. Was Banner correct? Explain.

31 Bankruptcy and Debt Adjustment

Chapter Outline

31-1 Bankruptcy and the Constitution

A. Bankruptcy is _____
_____

B. The federal government receives jurisdiction over bankruptcy from _____
_____

C. The Bankruptcy Code is found in _____
_____

31-2 Ordinary Bankruptcy— Chapter 7, Bankruptcy Code

A. Ordinary bankruptcy can begin in two ways
1. _____
2. _____

B. An automatic suspension stops _____

C. The Bankruptcy Code allows debtors to exclude _____
_____
_____
_____

D. To maintain a maximum standard of living, debtors are allowed to exclude _____
_____
_____
_____

E. A debtor's debts are paid by a trustee in the following order:
1. _____
2. _____
3. _____
4. _____
5. _____
6. _____
7. _____

31-3 Reorganization— Chapter 11, Bankruptcy Code

A. Reorganization means _____
_____

B. Three qualities of a reorganization plan are
1. _____

2. _____

3. _____

31-4 Family Farmer Debt Adjustment— Chapter 12, Bankruptcy Code

A. A family farmer is _____

_____

B. A Chapter 12 plan must include four provisions

1. _____

2. _____

3. _____

4. _____

31-5 Adjustment of Debts— Chapter 13, Bankruptcy Code

A. Chapter 13 of the Bankruptcy Code permits _____

_____

_____

B. Debts that cannot be discharged under Chapter 13 are

1. _____

2. _____

3. _____

Legal Concepts

For each statement, write T *in the answer column if the statement is true or* F *if the statement is false.*

Answer

1. Both the federal government and the states have jurisdiction over bankruptcy proceedings.

1. _____

2. Under Chapter 7 of the Bankruptcy Code, debtors are compelled to sell most of their property and use the cash to pay off their creditors.

2. _____

3. Voluntary bankruptcy filings are not allowed under Chapter 7.

3. _____

4. An automatic suspension prohibits creditors from filing lawsuits against the debtor.

4. *T*

5. Debtors can exclude a maximum of $4,000 for any individual item of household goods.

5. *F*

6. The Bankruptcy Code allows states to provide an alternate list of exemptions for debtors.

6. _____

7. Filing for bankruptcy does not allow a debtor to escape legal liability for any debt that arose from willful and malicious conduct.

7. _____

8. Debtors cannot discharge any cash advances that total more than $500 if those advances were obtained within 20 days of an order for relief.

8. _____

9. A Chapter 11 filing is available to anyone who is able to file under Chapter 7.

9. _____

10. Under Chapter 11, a business must cease operation before a reorganization plan can go into effect.

10. _____

11. A Chapter 11 primary committee consists of the debtor's unsecured debtors.

11. _____

12. A Chapter 11 reorganization plan requires unanimous approval by all creditors.

12. _____

13. To qualify for a Chapter 12 filing, 80 percent of a farmer's debt must result from nonfarm expenses.

13. _____

14. Individuals, corporations, partnerships, and sole proprietorships can all file under Chapter 13.

14. *F*

15. Under Chapter 13, the debtor must start payments within 30 days of submitting the plan to the court.

15. _____

Language of the Law

Select the legal term that best matches each definition.

a. automatic suspension
b. bankruptcy
c. bankruptcy trustee
d. confirmation
e. debtor-in-possession

f. discharge
g. family farmer
h. homestead exemption
i. liquidation
j. mortgage

k. order for relief
l. primary committee
m. reorganization
n. unimpaired class
o. waiver

Answer

1. A court's command to begin a bankruptcy proceeding
2. The individual charged with the responsibility of liquidating the assets of the debtor for the benefit of all interested parties
3. The elimination of the debtor's debts at the end of a bankruptcy proceeding
4. The legal process by which the assets of a debtor are sold to pay off creditors so that the debtor can make a fresh start financially
5. A stay that stops the debtor's creditors from making further moves to collect the money that the debtor owes them
6. Another name for ordinary bankruptcy
7. A group of creditors who work with a debtor to set up a reorganization plan
8. A group of creditors whose collection rights are not changed by a reorganization plan
9. A debtor who continues to run a business after filing a Chapter 11 reorganization petition
10. The official approval of a reorganization plan

1. _K_____
2. _C_____
3. _F_____
4. _B or I_
5. _A_____
6. _I_____
7. _L_____
8. _N_____
9. _E_____
10. _D_____

Applying the Law

1. Rodriquez owned a farm that had been badly undercapitalized from the start. After several years of operation, the financial condition of the farm was worse and several creditors decided to file an involuntary bankruptcy proceeding under Chapter 7. Rodriquez owed each of these creditors $2,500. Nevertheless, the involuntary petition was rejected. Why?

_____

_____

2. Bottaro was so deeply in debt that he decided to file for bankruptcy under Chapter 7. An order for relief was issued, and the automatic suspension went into effect. One of Bottaro's creditors, the Flores Department Store, filed a lawsuit against Bottaro in another court. The owners of the department store believed the suit would be allowed because they'd filed it in a court other than the one handling the bankruptcy. Were they correct? Explain.

_____

_____

3. Cutter filed for bankruptcy under Chapter 7. He decided to use his household exemption to protect his collection of expensive crystal. Taken all together, the complete collection was worth $7,500. However, each item, if listed separately, was worth $300, or $3,600 for 12 pieces of crystal. Advise Cutter on how to save the entire collection.

_____

_____

4. Newton filed for bankruptcy under Chapter 7. Rogers was appointed as trustee. Could Rogers be assured that she would be paid for her services even though Newton was bankrupt? Explain.

_____

_____

5. Knowing that he would have to file for bankruptcy on the following Monday, Simmons used his bank card on Friday night to take out a $2,000 cash advance. He then spent the money on several expensive items, believing that he would never have to pay back the entire cash advance. Was Simmons correct in this assumption? Why or why not?

_____

_____

6. Bennett and Cooper were partners in a family style restaurant that was having financial difficulties. The debts of the partnership were getting out of hand, and the partners knew they had to do something or they would lose the business. However, neither Bennett nor Cooper wanted to close down the business for good. Which chapter of the Bankruptcy Code should Bennett and Cooper file under? Why?

_____

_____

7. Corrales and Hennesey purchased a computer from St. Clair Electronics for their small corporation. The computer was purchased on credit. Corrales and Hennesey had to make monthly payments of $125.50 on the computer debt. St. Clair retained the right to repossess the computer should Corrales and Hennesey default. Corrales and Hennesey defaulted on three payments. They later filed for reorganization under Chapter 11. The owner of St. Clair argued that the electronics firm should be on the primary committee formed to work with Corrales and Hennesey. Was he correct? Why or why not?

_____

_____

8. Stephanski owned a 50 percent interest in a farm in Nebraska. Approximately 25 percent of her income was derived from this farm. The rest of her income came from a variety of other investments, as well as her full-time job. When she lost her job and several of her investments failed, Stephanski decided to file for debt adjustment as a farmer under Chapter 12. Was she able to do so? Why or why not?

_____

_____

9. Baron and Nadel were partners in a hardware store. Due to several unwise purchases, they found themselves faced with $90,000 in unsecured debts that they could not cover. When they decided to file for debt adjustment under Chapter 13, they were told that that chapter was not open to them. Why not?

_____

_____

10. Grant had overextended himself financially and, as a result, had failed to pay several unsecured debts. After attempting to collect these debts in a number of different ways, three of Grant's creditors joined forces and filed a petition for an involuntary debt adjustment proceeding under Chapter 13. Their request was turned down. Why?

_____

_____

32 The Principal and Agent Relationship

Chapter Outline

32-1 The Nature of the Agency Relationship

A. Agency is _____
_____

B. The parties involved in an agency relationship include
   1. _____
   2. _____

32-2 Agency as Distinguished from Other Relationships

A. The three kinds of principals are
   1. A disclosed principal is _____
   _____
   2. An undisclosed principal is _____
   _____
   3. A partially disclosed principal is _____
   _____

B. The two kinds of agents are
   1. A general agent is _____
   _____
   2. A special agent is _____

C. An independent contractor is _____
_____

32-3 Scope of the Agent's Authority

A. Express authority is _____
_____

B. Implied authority is _____
_____

C. Apparent authority is _____
_____

32-4 Creation of the Agency Relationship

A. An agency is created by _____
_____

B. Agency by implication may be created by _____
_____

C. Agency by necessity is created when _____
_____

D. Agency by operation of law is _____

_____

E. Agency by estoppel is created when _____

_____

F. Agency by ratification occurs when _____

_____

Legal Concepts

For each statement, write T *in the answer column if the statement is true or* F *if the statement is false.*

Answer

1. Agency relationships are always created as a result of a contract.   1. _____
2. When an agent is authorized to contract with third parties on behalf of a principal, the contract that the agent negotiates is between the principal and the third parties.   2. *T*____
3. Any person legally capable of entering into a contract may be a principal.   3. _____
4. An agent must always reveal the existence of a principal before entering into a contract with a third party.   4. *F*____
5. A minor cannot be an agent for an adult principal.   5. _____
6. An undisclosed principal is never liable on contracts made by an agent.   6. _____
7. When an agent is not known to be an agent and is acting as a principal, the agent can be held as a principal.   7. _____
8. A principal may cite the infancy of an agent as the reason for avoiding a contract made by that agent.   8. _____
9. Independent contractors are subject to the absolute control of the party they serve.   9. _____
10. Every partner in a partnership is an agent of that partnership.   10. _____
11. Express authority must always be put in writing by the principal.   11. _____
12. Once a principal has clothed an agent with apparent authority, the principal cannot deny that the authority exists.   12. _____
13. Agents can never delegate the authority given to them by their principals.   13. _____
14. A power of attorney can be made orally.   14. _____
15. The conduct of an agent alone cannot create an agency by estoppel.   15. _____

Language of the Law

Select the legal term that best matches each definition.

a. agency	**f.** general agent	**k.** principal
b. agent	**g.** implied authority	**l.** ratification
c. apparent authority	**h.** independent contractor	**m.** servant
d. disclosed principal	**i.** master	**n.** special agent
e. express authority	**j.** partially disclosed principal	**o.** undisclosed principal

Answer

1. A party who contracts to do a job for another party and who retains complete control over the methods employed to obtain completion of the job   1. *H*____
2. The authority of an agent to perform acts that are necessary or customary to carry out expressly authorized duties   2. *G*____
3. The principal's approval of previously unauthorized acts by an agent   3. *L*____
4. A person authorized to conduct a particular transaction only or to perform a specified act for the principal   4. *N*____
5. A legal agreement whereby one party is given the power to enter into transactions for the other party   5. *A*____

6. An accountability doctrine whereby a principal, by virtue of words or actions, leads a third party to believe that an agent has authority even though no authority was intended

7. Authority that a principal voluntarily and specifically sets forth as instructions in the agency agreement, orally or in writing

8. An individual authorized to act for another

9. A principal whose identity is known by third parties dealing through that principal's agent

10. An agent who is given broad authority to act on behalf of a principal and conduct the bulk of the principal's business on a daily basis

6. __C__

7. __E__

8. __B__

9. __D__

10. __F__

Applying the Law

1. Milton was recently hired to manage the Gibbons Dairy Farm. He was given the authority to hire and fire farmhands, buy and sell livestock, buy and sell machinery, supervise all milking operations, and make out the daily work schedule. Name and explain the type of agent that Milton's authority makes him.

_____

_____

_____

2. Tindle was hired by Fisher to attend an auction at the Swindell-Solik Art Gallery and to bid on a portrait of Ezra Pound that Fisher wanted very badly. Tindle had no authority to bid on any other art objects or to attend any other auctions. Name and explain the type of agent that Tindle's duties make her.

_____

_____

_____

3. Candiotti hired Davenport to sell Candiotti's new invention. This invention, called an inverter, was designed to triple the gas mileage of any automobile using unleaded gas. Davenport was given 10,000 inverters and a list of garages, repair shops, and auto shops to visit. At Mack's Used Car and Bike Shop in Shelby, Davenport sold 2,000 inverters to Mack Banyon on credit. When Banyon failed to pay for the inverters, Davenport was liable to Candiotti for the loss. Why?

_____

_____

_____

4. Snyder was hired as a traveling salesperson for the Neuman Florist Company. Snyder had the express authority to make contracts with customers and to deliver floral arrangements using the company truck. On one such delivery, the truck broke down and Snyder had to have it repaired. Name and explain the type of implied authority that allows Snyder to repair the truck.

_____

_____

_____

5. Harrigan hired Mullins, a minor, to act as his agent in the purchase of an automobile. After the sale was completed, Harrigan decided he no longer wanted the car. He tried to get out of the contract by arguing that Mullins was a minor and that contracts made by minors were voidable by the minor. Was Harrigan wrong? Explain.

_____

_____

_____

6. Cairo Steel, Inc., awarded a contract to Tri-State Shipping to transport a cargo of steel down the Mississippi River from St. Louis to New Orleans. While on the river, the Tri-State barge collided with a barge owned by Newton Transport, causing heavy damage to the Newton ship. Tri-State owned all its own barges and exercised complete control over the loading and transport of all cargo. Nevertheless, Newton sued both Tri-State and Cairo Steel for the damage to Newton's barge. Was Cairo liable to Newton? Explain.

_____

_____

7. Phelps, a rich and famous movie star, was in the market for a new house. Realizing that buyers would raise the prices of their homes when they knew he was the prospective buyer, Phelps hired Jenkins to act as his agent. Phelps told Jenkins he could reveal that he was an agent but could not reveal Phelps's identity to any potential sellers. Name and explain the type of principal Phelps had become.

_____

_____

8. Louden worked as a part-time clerk for the Province State Insurance Company. As a part-time clerk, she had no power to bind the company to insurance contracts. Nevertheless, she sold an automobile insurance policy to Carothers. For two years, Carothers made payments that were accepted by Province State. When Carothers had an accident and tried to collect from Province State, the company told him that Louden never had the authority to enter into the contract in the first place. Was the company correct? Why or why not?

_____

_____

9. Cayne was about to go on a round-the-world cruise that would last six months. However, he had some real property that he was trying to sell, and he did not want to wait for six months to find a buyer. Consequently, he called his daughter, Julia, and told her she had the power to sell the land while he was away. After Cayne had gone on the cruise, Julia found out that she could not sell Cayne's land. Why not?

_____

_____

10. Bosworth received notice to appear at the county courthouse on Monday morning to perform jury duty. Since Bosworth was scheduled to leave on vacation that Monday, he appointed Cheever to act as his agent on the jury. Was the appointment valid? Explain.

_____

_____

_____

33 Operation and Termination of Agency

Chapter Outline

33-1 Agents' Obligations to Principal

A. Agents have the following obligations to their principals:

1. _____
2. _____
3. _____
4. _____
5. _____
6. _____

B. When an agent fails to observe a duty owed to a principal, the principal has the following remedies available:

1. _____
2. _____
3. _____
4. _____
5. _____
6. _____
7. _____

33-2 Principal's Obligations to Agent

A. The principal has the following obligations to the agent:

1. _____
2. _____
3. _____
4. _____

B. When a principal fails to observe a duty owed to an agent, the agent has the following remedies available:

1. _____
2. _____
3. _____
4. _____
5. _____

33-3 Tort and Criminal Liability in an Agency

A. Tort liability involves the following principles:

1. *Respondeat superior* is _____
_____

2. Sovereign immunity is _____
_____

B. A principal can be held liable for an agent's crimes in the following situations:

1. _____
2. _____
3. _____
4. _____

33-4 Termination of Agency

A. An agency may be terminated by acts of the parties in the following ways:

1. _____
2. _____
3. _____

B. An agency may be terminated by operation of law under the following circumstances:

1. _____
2. _____
3. _____
4. _____

Legal Concepts

For each statement, write T *in the answer column if the statement is true or* F *if the statement is false.*

Answer

1. An agent may not enter into any agency transaction in which the agent has a personal interest.

   1. _____

2. Only agents who are paid for their agency activities are required to obey all reasonable and legal instructions issued by the principal.

   2. _____

3. An agent may not engage in any activity that would result in a conflict of interest with the business of the principal.

   3. _____

4. Money collected by an agent for a principal may be temporarily commingled with the agent's own funds.

   4. _____

5. In the absence of authority to do so, an agent may not delegate duties to others unless such duties require no particular knowledge, training, skill, or responsibility.

   5. _____

6. The agent is bound by duty to keep the principal fully informed of all facts that materially affect the subject matter of the agency.

   6. _____

7. An agent may not recover compensation for illegal services unless they were rendered at the request of the principal.

   7. _____

8. Agents cannot recover for expenses that arise from their own negligence.

   8. _____

9. Agents are entitled to indemnification if they incur a loss or are damaged as a result of a principal's request.

   9. _T_____

10. When an agent or employee causes harm to a third person, the principal or employer is ordinarily not liable for that harm.

    10. _F_____

11. Sovereign immunity remains an important defense for torts committed by the government.

    11. _____

12. The U.S. Supreme Court has barred virtually all damage suits against the federal government for injuries to military personnel.

    12. _____

13. The principal is always liable for an agent's crimes.

    13. _____

14. The insanity of the principal, but not that of the agent, will usually terminate the authority of the agent.

    14. _____

15. The principal is not required to notify third parties of the agency's termination if the agency has ended by operation of law.

    15. _____

Language of the Law

Select the legal term that best matches each definition.

a. commingled
b. cooperation
c. duty to account
d. good cause
e. gratuitous agent

f. indemnification
g. intent
h. personal service
i. recovery
j. renunciation

k. *respondeat superior*
l. revocation
m. scope of authority
n. sovereign immunity
o. vicarious liability

Answer

1. Payment to the agent for loss or damage suffered in carrying out the principal's business
2. The principal's duty to refrain from interfering in the agent's ability to perform his or her assigned tasks
3. The range of acts an agent can perform while doing his or her job for the principal
4. The obligation that agents have to keep the principal's money separate from their own and to report to the principal on the status of that money
5. The concept of laying responsibility upon one person for the actions of another
6. A doctrine that prevents a lawsuit from arising against the government without the government's consent
7. A termination of an agency by the principal's revoking the agent's authority to act
8. A failure on the part of an agent to keep the principal's funds separate from the agent's funds
9. A substantial or legally sufficient reason for doing something
10. A termination of an agency by the agent's giving notice to the principal that he or she is quitting

1. _____
2. _____
3. _____
4. _____
5. _____
6. _____
7. _____
8. _____
9. _____
10. _____

Applying the Law

1. Perez hired Hunter to act as a clerk in his hardware store. Perez instructed Hunter to sell on a cash basis only. When DeFazio, a regular customer at the hardware store, asked Hunter if she could purchase a lawn mower on credit, Hunter agreed. When Perez found out, he discharged Hunter. Was Perez within his rights to do so? Explain.

_____

_____

2. Adams was hired as a purchasing agent for Klein's shoe store. Using his own money, Adams purchased a load of shoes from the manufacturer. He then re-sold the shoes to Klein's at an enormous profit. Name and explain the duty Adams violated here.

_____

_____

3. Mazzeo worked as a door-to-door salesperson for the Ranger Outback Book Company. In this capacity, he frequently collected money from his sales. One week he carelessly deposited some of Ranger's money in his own bank account. When he tried to retrieve the money, he could no longer remember how much of the money belonged to Ranger and how much was his own. What legal remedy does Ranger have here?

_____

_____

4. Hegel, a financial expert with an international reputation, was hired to manage the financial affairs of O'Hara. Hegel hired a recent college graduate and delegated the management of O'Hara's money to him. May O'Hara refuse to honor this arrangement? Why or why not?

_____

_____

_____

5. Brooks was hired as a purchasing agent for McGuire's electronics firm. Frye, a salesperson for Southern Cross Electronics, told Brooks that the electronic components he wanted to purchase had recently doubled in price. Brooks went ahead and purchased the component parts anyway. When McGuire learned about the price change, he refused to honor the contract. Could Southern Cross sue McGuire for breach of contract? Explain.

_____

_____

_____

6. While on a business trip to New York for General Spectrum Enterprises, Ballew attended a Broadway play. When Ballew sought reimbursement for the price of the play tickets, General Spectrum refused to honor the request. Was General Spectrum acting correctly? Explain.

_____

_____

_____

7. Fegley hired Mesher to sell an antique statuette to Snavely. Fegley cautioned Mesher not to reveal to Snavely that he worked for Fegley. After the sale was complete, Snavely discovered that the statuette was a forgery. He sued Mesher and recovered the purchase price. What were Mesher's rights in this situation?

_____

_____

_____

8. Dowell was hired as a salesperson for Karan. As part of his duties, he was required to travel throughout the city contacting all of his assigned clients. On one such trip, he ran a stop sign and collided with Jameston's car, injuring her and damaging her vehicle. When Jameston discovered Dowell worked for Karan, she included Karan in a negligence suit arising from the accident. What legal principle allowed her to do this? Explain.

_____

_____

_____

9. Tackett worked as a purchasing agent for Unicorn Industries. Because of certain company policies, he was required to make purchases with his own funds. The company them reimbursed him for those purchases. When Tackett filed for bankruptcy, he was told that his agency relationship with Unicorn had terminated. Explain.

_____

_____

_____

10. Wilder hired Egan to sell Wilder's private jet. Before any sale could be made, the jet was destroyed by terrorists. The destruction of the jet terminated the agency relationship. Who must Wilder inform of the termination?

_____

_____

_____

34 Employment Law

Chapter Outline

34-1 The Employment Relationship

A. The doctrine of employment-at-will means _____
_____

B. A collective bargaining agreement is _____

C. People who can negotiate their own individual professional employment contracts
include _____

D. Several theories have been developed by state courts to limit employment-at-will.
They include

1. _____

2. _____

3. _____

34-2 Laws Regulating Employment Conditions

A. The Occupational Safety and Health Administration (OSHA) establishes _____

B. The Fair Labor Standards Act provides _____

C. The Immigration Reform Act of 1986 created _____

34-3 Worker Benefits

A. Under the Federal Insurance Contributions Act, both employers and employees are
_____

B. The unemployment insurance section of the Social Security Acts provides for
_____

C. State workers' compensation laws compensate workers or their dependents for
_____

D. The federal Employee Retirement Income Security Act of 1974 (ERISA) provides
_____

34-4 Equal Employment Opportunity

A. The Civil Rights Act of 1964 prohibits _____

B. The Civil Rights Act of 1992 was enacted to meet several objectives. Two of these are

1. _____

2. _____

C. The Age Discrimination in Employment Act prohibits _____

D. The primary objective of the Vietnam Era Veterans Readjustment Act (VEVRA) is
_____

E. The Americans with Disabilities Act is designed to _____
_____
_____

Legal Concepts

For each statement, write T *in the answer column if the statement is true or* F *if the statement is false.*

1. Only written contracts can create an employment relationship.
2. Under a grievance procedure, employees have the right to appeal an employer's decision that they thought was unjust.
3. Wrongful discharge gives employees legal ground for a lawsuit against employers who have dismissed them unfairly.
4. Implied contract is the only ground recognized by the courts for a wrongful discharge lawsuit.
5. OSHA establishes federal health and safety standards for the workplace.
6. Learners, apprentices, and messengers can be employed for less than the minimum wage.
7. The unemployment insurance section of the Social Security Act provides for a joint federal and state system of unemployment insurance.
8. State workers' compensation laws compensate workers or their dependents for injuries, disease, or death that occurs on the job or as a result of it.
9. Under current state workers' compensation statutes, the common law defenses that were used by employers are no longer effective.
10. The Civil Rights Act of 1964 prohibits discrimination based on sex, race, color, national origin, and religion.
11. The only type of discrimination is disparate treatment.
12. A bona fide occupational qualification can be used by an employer as a defense against a charge of disparate treatment.
13. The Civil Rights Act of 1992 expands the availability of compensatory but not punitive damages.
14. The Age Discrimination in Employment Act protects workers between the ages of 25 and 39.
15. The Americans with Disabilities Act does not define disability.

1. F
2. ____
3. ____
4. ____
5. T
6. ____
7. ____
8. ____
9. ____
10. T
11. ____
12. F
13. ____
14. ____
15. F

Language of the Law

Select the legal term that best matches each definition.

a. collective bargaining agreement
b. disability
c. disclaimer
d. disparate impact
e. disparate treatment
f. employment-at-will
g. grievance procedure
h. implied contract
i. implied covenant
j. workers' compensation
k. wrongful discharge

1. Indirect discrimination
2. A clause in an employment application or manual designed to preserve employment-at-will
3. The wrongful discharge theory that holds that there is an implied promise of fairness and honesty in all employment relationships
4. A system that compensates workers or their dependents for injuries, disease, or death that occurs on the job or as a result of it
5. Deliberate discrimination
6. A legal theory that gives employees legal grounds for a lawsuit against employers who have dismissed them unfairly
7. The legal theory that holds that an employer can discharge an employee at any time for any reason with or without notice
8. Any physical or mental impairment that substantially limits one or more of the major life activities

1. D
2. C
3. I
4. J
5. E
6. K
7. F
8. B

9. A procedure that gives employees the right to appeal an employer's decision that they think is unjust

9. __G__

10. A contract negotiated between an employer and a labor union

10. __A__

Applying the Law

1. Jack Garfield worked as a bank teller for the Farmers' Savings and Loan. Although he was a loyal and competent worker, he was discharged so that the head of the S & L could give the job to someone else. Garfield was an at-will employee. Under the doctrine of employment-at-will, what were Garfield's legal rights?

_____
_____
_____

2. Edward Samuels worked as an electrician for The Delaware Electrical Supply Corporation. He was also a member of the United Electrical Workers of America (UEWA). Samuels was discharged when he reported for work late. The collective bargaining agreement between Delaware and the UEWA forbid the discharge of an employee for a single incidence of lateness. Any violations were to be in writing and workers were to be given a second chance. What recourse did Samuels have? Explain.

_____
_____
_____

3. Maria Morley, who worked for the Heisenberg Research Corporation, took a leave of absence for health reasons. Her supervisor, Gary Planck, told Morley, "When your medical problem is cured, you can have your job back with full seniority." Morley believed Planck and did not look for employment elsewhere. When she returned to work, Morley found that Heisenberg would not honor Planck's promise. It took Morley six months to find a job. Did Morley have any legal recourse? Explain.

_____
_____
_____

4. Carol Hawkins applied for a job as a physicist with the VonBraun Research Corporation. The employee handbook included a disclaimer that said that employees could be discharged with or without notice at any time for any reason and even without a reason. Only the president of VonBraun could alter this provision. Hawkins, who had other job prospects lined up, told Werner Goddard, who wanted to hire Hawkins, that she would not work under such a provision. Goddard told her to ignore the disclaimer and promised Hawkins a job for life. Was Goddard's promise legally effective? Explain.

_____
_____
_____

5. Jim Hubble was to receive a 10 percent commission on all sales he made for his employer, the Radical Computer Corporation. Hubble sold a $10 million computer system to the NASA for a new orbiting laboratory. To avoid paying $1 million to Hubble, Radical fired him, despite his record as an excellent salesperson. Hubble's state recognizes the implied covenant theory of wrongful discharge. Explain the legal rights that this theory would give to Hubble.

_____
_____
_____

6. Lisa Hegel, a respiratory therapist, was laid off from her job with the Akron City Center Hospital because of economic conditions. She registered with the state unemployment compensation agency and requested unemployment compensation. The interviewing official told her about a job opening for a respiratory therapist at the Canton Clinic. Hegel refused it on the grounds that she needed a vacation before accepting another job. Would Hegel qualify for unemployment compensation? Explain.

_____

_____

_____

7. The *Fashion Leader,* a magazine that featured women's fashions, advertised for female models for a special swimwear issue. Explain why such a hiring practice would not violate the Civil Rights Act of 1964.

_____

_____

_____

8. Yulanda Uttermeyer, aged 62, lost her position when the subsidiary she worked for was disbanded by the Hume Petrochemical Corporation, the parent corporation. All of the employees who were laid off as a result of the closing were promised preferential treatment for other jobs at Hume. Uttermeyer applied for over 50 of these positions. She was never rehired. The reason given for her rejection was that she was overqualified. Uttermeyer believed that she could bring an age discrimination suit under the ADEA. Was she correct? Explain.

_____

_____

_____

9. Jeffrey Hofstetler was employed by the Comestock Corporation. He also was an army reservist attached to a transportation corps battalion that was activated to serve in Operation Desert Shield and Operation Desert Storm. Hofstetler believed that under the terms of the Vietnam Era Veterans Act, as long as Comestock held a contract with the federal government, the corporation would be required to apply its internal leave of absence policies to Hofstetler's situation. He also believed that if he were dissatisfied with the way he was treated by Comestock then he could take his complaint to the Veteran's Employment Service (VES). Was he correct? Explain.

_____

_____

_____

10. Georgette MacKay has a visual disability. She applied for a position as an accountant with the Daystrom Corporation. Frederick Hansen, the human resources director, tested her eyesight by having her read several documents in very fine print. MacKay failed the test and, on that basis alone, was rejected. MacKay believed that Daystrom violated the ADA. Was she correct? Explain.

_____

_____

_____

35 Labor-Management Relations Law

Chapter Outline

35-1 Source of Labor-Management Relations

A. A labor union is _____
_____

B. The three aims of labor unions are
1. _____
2. _____
3. _____

35-2 Major Federal Labor Legislation

A. The Clayton Act prohibited federal courts from _____
_____

B. The Railway Labor Act provided procedures for _____
_____

C. The Norris-LaGuardia Act specified acts that were not subject to federal court injunction. These acts included
1. _____
2. _____
3. _____

D. The Norris-LaGuardia Act also outlawed _____
_____

E. The National Labor Relations Act (the Wagner Act) gave workers the right to
_____

F. The Wagner Act also created _____
_____

G. The Taft-Hartley Act established _____
_____

H. The Landrum-Griffin Act is designed to _____
_____

35-3 Collective Bargaining Process

A. The National Labor Relations Board (NLRB) is _____
_____

B. The NLRB has exclusive jurisdiction to _____
_____

C. Arbitration involves _____
_____

D. The federal Mediation and Conciliation Service was formed to _____
_____

A. Strikes in the public sector by police, fire fighters, refuse collectors, air traffic controllers, and postal workers are _____

_____

B. The U.S. Supreme Court has affirmed lower court rulings that _____

_____

Legal Concepts

For each statement, write T *in the answer column if the statement is true or* F *if the statement is false.*

Answer

1. Union organizing activities are protected by federal and state laws, as well as by the U.S. Constitution.

   1. _____
2. The first federal statute relating to labor was the Taft-Hartley Act.

   2. _____
3. The Railway Labor Act does not deal with the airline industry.

   3. _____
4. The Norris-LaGuardia Act gave the federal courts the power to grant injunctions prohibiting striking, picketing, and boycotting.

   4. __F__
5. The Wagner Act gave workers the right to organize, join, and aid labor unions.

   5. __T__
6. The Taft-Hartley Act created the NLRB.

   6. __F__
7. Under the Wagner Act, employers are permitted to reward workers who do not participate in union activities.

   7. _____
8. The Taft-Hartley Act includes a free speech provision that allows employers to comment more freely on union organizing activities.

   8. _____
9. Under the Wagner Act, employers are permitted to form company-run unions as long as they follow the union certification procedures.

   9. _____
10. The Wagner Act permits closed shop agreements between the employer and the union.

    10. _____
11. Unions can set rules for their internal operation and can punish union members who disobey those rules.

    11. _____
12. The Taft-Hartley Act permits only secondary boycotts.

    12. _____
13. The Landrum-Griffin Act established a "bill of rights" to allow employees to participate in certain selected union procedures.

    13. _____
14. Decisions by the NLRB may be appealed to the appropriate U.S. Court of Appeals and then to the Supreme Court.

    14. _____
15. In the public sector, strikes by employees performing vital services are generally illegal unless specifically authorized by statute.

    15. _____

Language of the Law

Select the legal term that best matches each definition.

a. bargaining unit
b. boycott
c. closed shop
d. collective bargaining
e. constructive discharge

f. featherbedding
g. hot-cargo contract
h. labor union
i. picketing
j. right-to-work laws

k. secondary boycott
l. strike
m. unfair labor practice
n. union shop
o. yellow-dog contracts

Answer

1. An agreement in which an employer agrees with a union not to handle, use, or deal in the non-union-produced goods of another employer

   1. __G__
2. Keeping unneeded employees, paying employees for not working, or assigning more employees than needed to a given job

   2. __F__
3. State laws that prohibit labor-management agreements requiring union membership as a condition of getting or keeping a job

   3. __J__

4. A place of employment where nonunion workers may be employed for a trial period of not more than 30 days after which nonunion workers must join the union or be discharged

5. An improper employment practice by either an employer or a union

6. A stoppage of work by employees as a means of enforcing a demand made on their employer

7. A good faith meeting between employers and representatives of employees to discuss the terms and conditions of employment

8. An organization of employees that acts on behalf of all employees of a particular group in negotiations with the employer regarding the terms of their employment

9. The placement of persons for observation, patrol, and demonstration at the site of employment as part of employee pressure on an employer to meet employee demands

10. A work site in which the employer, by agreement, hires only union members in good standing

4. _N_

5. _m_

6. _L_

7. _D_

8. _H_

9. _I_

10. _C_

Applying the Law

1. Wheaton owned and operated Wheaton's Wheat Shop, a bakery with four stores. When Wheaton found out that his employees were planning to form a union, he sent out a memo that said that any employee who joined the union would be disciplined and very likely discharged. Did such a memo violate federal law? Explain.

_____

_____

_____

2. Holland ran a chain of jewelry stores located in several different cities in Ohio, Michigan, and Indiana. When he found out that his employees were organizing a union, he sent out a memo that promised 10 percent pay raises to any employee who refused to join the union. Did Holland's actions violate federal law? Explain.

_____

_____

_____

3. Avery owned and operated a chain of health spas throughout the South. When she learned that Douglas, one of the employees in her Augusta, Georgia store, was talking about forming a union, she transferred him to Savannah and demoted him from supervisor to sales clerk. The move meant a loss of seniority for Douglas, and the demotion meant a pay cut and a loss of authority. What illegal employment practice did Avery use in this situation? Explain.

_____

_____

_____

4. Bishop Stanford was approached by the faculty of several religious schools under his jurisdiction. The faculty members declared that they had started a union. They further demanded that the bishop engage in a collective bargaining session with them. The faculty members concluded their dicussion by indicating their intent to take the matter to the NLRB should the bishop refuse their demands. Could the faculty members do this? Explain.

_____

_____

_____

5. Carlyle ran a chain of sporting goods stores in Georgia, Alabama, and Florida. One of Carlyle's employees informed him that his workers were planning to form a union. To head off this attempt, Carlyle set up a company-run union. She later learned that such a tactic was illegal. Explain.

_____

_____

6. Langhorne was president of the Montana and Idaho Book Binding Company. Edwards, an employee of Montana and Idaho, told Langhorne that the employees wanted to form a union. Upon learning of this plan, Langhorne called a meeting to explain his point of view on the effects of unionizing. Edwards told Langhorne that such a meeting was illegal. Was Edwards correct? Explain.

_____

_____

7. Union representatives and corporate officers of the Fairfax Tire Company met in a collective bargaining session to negotiate a new contract. As part of the new contract, the union representatives demanded that 12 people be added to each shift even though they knew only eight people were needed. Corporate officials, confident of their position, correctly refused to comply with the request. Why?

_____

_____

8. Mulligan, a new member of the Federated International Workers Union, asked to speak at the next union meeting. Gleason, president of the union, told Mulligan that he would have to be a union member for five years before he would be allowed to speak at union meetings. Was Gleason correct? Explain.

_____

_____

9. Catlin owned and operated the Hapwood Corporation, which had stores in West Virginia, Pennsylvania, and Kentucky. When he found out that union members were forcing workers to join the union, he threatened to file a notice with the NLRB. Keene, a union official, argued that only union members could file notice with the NLRB. Was Keene correct? Explain.

_____

_____

10. Employees of the U.S. Defense Department, unhappy over low wages, decided to strike. When a federal court ordered the strikers back to work, they refused to obey, citing their constitutional right to strike. The strikers were fired, and the union was fined. Explain this result.

_____

_____

_____

36 Partnership

Chapter Outline

36-1 Partnership Characteristics

A. A partnership is _____

_____

B. The two essential elements of a partnership are

1. _____

2. _____

36-2 Partnership Formation

A. Three primary items that should be in a written partnership agreement are

1. _____

2. _____

3. _____

B. A person may receive a share of profits and avoid the label of "partner" if the share is paid as

1. _____

2. _____

3. _____

4. _____

5. _____

36-3 The Acquisition of Partnership Property

To determine whether property belongs to a partnership or to one of its partners, the court may ask the following questions:

A. _____

B. _____

C. _____

D. _____

E. _____

36-4 Partner Rights, Duties, and Liabilities

A. Tenancy in partnership has the following characteristics:

1. _____

2. _____

3. _____

4. _____

5. _____

B. A partner's interest in the partnership is _____

_____

C. All partners have _____ rights in the management of the partnership.

36-5 Dissolution of a
Partnership

Partnerships dissolve in three ways

A. _____

B. _____

C. _____

36-6 Limited
Partnerships

A. A limited partnership is _____

_____

B. Limited liability means _____

_____

Legal Concepts

For each statement, write T *in the answer column if the statement is true or* F *if the statement is false.*

Answer

1. Partnerships must involve at least three persons.
2. The sharing of profits is considered *prima facie* evidence of the existence of a partnership.
3. Regardless of the way profits are shared, losses are always shared equally.
4. A partner's individual nonpartnership property can be used to pay partnership debts even before the partnership runs out of money.
5. Partnership agreements can never be oral.
6. A person can avoid the label "partner" if the share of profits he or she receives is paid as wages.
7. Partnership by estoppel creates a true partnership.
8. Capital contributions are considered the property of the partnership.
9. If a dispute arises as to whether a piece of property belongs to the partnership or to a partner, the court will award it to the partnership.
10. A partner's tenancy in partnership rights may not be assigned to a nonpartner unless the other partner consents.
11. A partner's interest in his or her share of profits may not be assigned to a nonpartner unless the other partners consent.
12. Management rights are proportioned among partners according to their capital contributions.
13. Partnership books must be kept at the partnership's principal place of business and must be available for the inspection of all the partners.
14. Bankruptcy of an individual partner causes a dissolution of a partnership by operation of law.
15. A failure to file a certificate of limited partnership will always deprive a limited partner of limited liability.

1. _F_
2. _T_
3. ___
4. _F_
5. ___
6. ___
7. ___
8. ___
9. ___
10. ___
11. _F_
12. ___
13. _T_
14. ___
15. ___

Language of the Law

Select the legal term that best matches each definition.

a. accounting
b. annuity
c. articles of partnership
d. assigned
e. attachment

f. capital
g. capital contributions
h. dissolution of a partnership
i. limited partnership
j. partnership

k. partnership by estoppel
l. *prima facie* evidence
m. reserve funds
n. surplus
o. tenancy in partnership

Answer

1. Sums contributed by partners as permanent investment to the partnership
2. Net assets of a partnership
3. Each partner's property interest in specific items of partnership property

1. _G_
2. _F_
3. _O_

4. Any funds that remain after a partnership has been dissolved and all other debts have been settled

4. ___N___

5. An association of two or more persons to carry on a business for a profit

5. ___J___

6. The written agreement that establishes a partnership

6. ___C___

7. A guaranteed retirement income

7. ___B___

8. A partnership that is created when an individual says or does something that leads a third party to the reasonable belief that the partnership exists

8. ___K___

9. A partnership formed by two or more persons having one or more general and one or more limited partners

9. ___I___

10. A statement detailing the financial transactions of a partnership and the status of its assets

10. ___A___

Applying the Law

1. Cooke and Corbin formed a partnership to sell tires for trucks and automobiles. They leased a warehouse from Strong and paid him rent of $1,000 per month. When the partnership dissolved, Strong claimed he was a partner because he'd shared in Cooke's and Corbin's profits. Was Strong wrong? Explain.

_____
_____
_____

2. Foster and Banner were partners in a printing business. They purchased several hundred gallons of ink from the Silvermine Ink Corporation. When they had difficulty paying their bills, an attorney for Silvermine told Foster that the corporation was going to try to force him to sell his car to pay for the ink. At this point in time, Silvermine will be unable to do this. Why?

_____
_____
_____

3. Rooney and Sargent entered into an oral partnership agreement to purchase several thousand acres of ranchland in Wyoming. Rooney later backed out of the agreement, claiming that it was unenforceable. Was he correct? Explain.

_____
_____
_____

4. Harrigan and Russell were partners in a music store. Harrigan owed Galt $1,500 on a personal debt. Galt had threatened to go to court to force the partnership to sell its computer to satisfy Harrigan's personal debt to him. Would Galt be able to do this? Explain.

_____
_____
_____

5. Hawkens, Cohen, and Newton were partners in a drugstore. Hawkens decided to assign his share of the profits to his daughter. Cohen and Newton claimed that this action would dissolve the partnership. Were they correct? Explain.

_____
_____
_____

6. Robinson, Lopez, and Curren were partners in a bookstore. Robinson felt that they should purchase a computer for the store. Lopez and Curren disagreed. Robinson purchased the computer anyway. He then asked Lopez and Curren to reimburse him for the money he spent on the computer system, which they refused to do. Was their refusal legally correct? Explain.

_____

_____

7. Ricardo, Orwell, and Pembroke voted to make Radford a new partner in their firm. Simpson, a fourth partner, objected to the admission of Radford. Ricardo, Orwell, and Pembroke argued that Simpson's lone dissenting vote did not matter because they had a majority on their side. Were they correct? Explain.

_____

_____

8. Wong and Blum were partners in a clothing store. While on a routine delivery, Blum caused an accident when he ran a stoplight. Wong claimed that only Blum would be liable for the injuries sustained by the other driver. Was Wong correct? Explain.

_____

_____

9. As partners, O'Connor and Welsh ran a dry-cleaning business. After five years, it became clear that the business could be carried on only at a loss. O'Connor wanted to shut down operations. Welsh did not. O'Connor argued that since the partnership could be operated only at a loss, it was dissolved by operation of law. Was O'Connor correct? Explain.

_____

_____

10. Fletcher was the limited partner and Harkins the general partner in the Green Lawn and Supply Emporium. Schaps knew Fletcher was supposed to be a limited partner. However, when Schaps filed suit against Green to recover a debt, he named Fletcher as a party to the suit because Schaps had found out that a certificate of limited partnership had not been filed. Nevertheless, Schaps's addition of Fletcher to the suit was incorrect. Why?

_____

_____

_____

37 Corporate Formation and Finance

Chapter Outline

37-1 The Nature of the Corporation

A. A corporation is _____

_____

B. Under provisions of the U.S. Constitution, a corporation is considered _____

_____

37-2 Types of Corporations

A. A private corporation is _____

_____

B. A public corporation is _____

_____

C. A quasi-public corporation is _____

_____

D. A close corporation is _____

_____

E. An S corporation is _____

37-3 Formation of the Corporation

A. Promoters are _____

_____

B. Incorporators are _____

_____

C. The articles of incorporation are _____

_____

37-4 Defective Incorporation

A. A *de jure* corporation is _____

_____

B. A *de facto* corporation requires the following conditions

1. _____

2. _____

3. _____

C. A corporation by estoppel is _____

37-5 Piercing the Corporate Veil

A. The courts use the doctrine of piercing the corporate veil to _____

_____

B. Shareholders of close corporations fall victim to piercing the corporate veil because

_____

A. Common stock is _____

B. Preferred stock is _____

C. Par value is _____

D. No par value stock is _____

E. Cash dividends are _____

F. Stock dividends are _____

Legal Concepts

For each statement, write T *in the answer column if the statement is true or* F *if the statement is false.*

Answer

1. As a legal entity, a corporation can own property but can neither sue nor be sued.

   1. _F_

2. Within the meaning of the Fourteenth Amendment, a corporation may not be deprived of life, liberty, or property without due process of law.

   2. _____

3. A corporation is considered to be a citizen of only the state in which it is incorporated.

   3. _____

4. Private corporations can be organized for profit or for nonprofit purposes.

   4. _T_

5. Corporations that are privately organized for profit cannot provide services upon which the public is dependent.

   5. _____

6. Promoters have a fiduciary relationship with the not-yet-existent corporation and its future shareholders.

   6. _____

7. A foreign corporation need not obtain a certificate of authority to transport goods across a host state.

   7. _____

8. Promoters have no power to bind a corporation to a contract until that corporation has been formed.

   8. _____

9. The courts will prevent a duplication of corporate names if such duplication causes confusion or unfair competition.

   9. _____

10. A *de facto* corporation has the same rights, privileges, and duties as a *de jure* corporation as far as the state is concerned.

    10. _____

11. Piercing the corporate veil applies to large corporations only.

    11. _____

12. Corporation by estoppel creates a real corporation.

    12. _____

13. Holders of common stock are guaranteed to receive dividends quarterly.

    13. _____

14. All states have authorized corporations to issue stock with no par value.

    14. _____

15. The most common kind of dividend is the cash dividend.

    15. _____

Language of the Law

Select the legal term that best matches each definition.

a. bylaws
b. certificate of authority
c. certificate of incorporation
d. close corporation
e. common stock

f. corporation
g. corporation by estoppel
h. *de facto* corporation
i. *de jure* corporation
j. dividends

k. pierce the corporate veil
l. preferred stock
m. promoters
n. statutory agent
o. stock certificate

Answer

1. Net profits or surplus set aside for the shareholders of a corporation

   1. _____

2. A document that grants a foreign corporation permission to do business in another state

   2. _____

3. The corporation's official authorization to do business in the state of incorporation

   3. _____

4. An individual who is designated to receive service of process when a lawsuit is filed against the corporation

   4. _____

5. A corporation whose existence is the result of the incorporator's having fully or substantially complied with the relevant incorporation statutes

   5. _____

6. A legal entity created by either a state or federal statute authorizing individuals to operate an enterprise

6. __F__

7. Rules that guide the corporation's day-to-day internal affairs

7. _____

8. Written evidence of the ownership of a unit of interest in the corporation

8. _____

9. A class of stock that has rights over other classes of stock

9. _____

10. The people who do the actual day-to-day work involved in the incorporation process

10. __m__

Applying the Law

1. Dynasoar, Inc., was incorporated in Delaware and had its principal place of business in New Jersey. The directors of Dynasoar decided to open a branch office and several stores in Mississippi. What legal steps will Dynasoar have to take before opening either the office or the stores?

_____

_____

2. Tolliver, Mueller, and Dwyer were shareholders and directors of TMD, Inc. Tolliver and Mueller wanted to declare S corporation status. Dwyer objected. Tolliver and Mueller convinced the other 40 shareholders to go along with their plan. Nevertheless, Dwyer still claimed that TMD could not declare S corporation status. Was Dwyer correct? Explain.

_____

_____

3. Hayes acted as promoter in the incorporation of the Dry-by-Night Cleaning Company. As part of the process of forming Dry-by-Night, Hayes purchased a delivery van from the Eaton Auto Mall. The effort to incorporate Dry-by-Night failed, and Hayes was forced to pay for the van himself. Why?

_____

_____

4. McKinley, Hinders, and Manning followed all the correct steps in the incorporation process. However, after filing with the secretary of state's office, their papers were lost and a certificate of incorporation was never issued. Nevertheless, they operated as if they were a corporation. When one of their drivers caused an automobile accident, McKinley, Hinders, and Manning were sued as individuals rather than as a corporation. Identify and explain the doctrine they can use in their defense.

_____

_____

_____

5. Phillips did everything that was necessary under state law to incorporate. However, he continued to run his business as a sole proprietorship and simply used the false corporate front to avoid personal liability on several contracts entered into for personal reasons but in the corporation's name. One of Phillips's creditors decided to disregard the phony corporate front and sue Phillips directly. Identify the legal theory that allowed the creditor to do this.

_____

_____

_____

6. Riley was asked to invest in New Markets. He was told that New Markets was a legally formed corporation; in fact, no incorporation had ever taken place. Later, Riley was asked to become vice-president of New Markets. As part of his job, he ordered the purchase of several computers from Kearney Komputers, Inc. When New Markets failed to pay for the computers and Kearney found out that the corporation did not really exist, Kearney attempted to hold Riley personally liable. Identify the legal doctrine that might protect Riley in this case.

_____

_____

_____

7. Zelek, Inc., was incorporated in Delaware and had its principal place of business in Maryland. Zelek had no holdings in any other states and did business exclusively in Maryland. The Lennons had an automobile accident with a Zelek delivery truck while they were visiting relatives in Maryland. They then returned to Virginia and attempted to sue Zelek in Virginia. Their attempt failed. Why?

_____

_____

_____

8. Enright owned 100 shares of common stock in Antares, Inc. In five years he had received no dividend payments. As a result, he elected to sue Antares, claiming that the directors had a duty to pay dividends at least once every year. Was Enright correct? Explain.

_____

_____

_____

9. Marple and Taft were both shareholders in Radnik, Inc. For two years neither of them received dividends. In the third year both received dividends. Marple also received payment for dividends not paid in the previous two years. Taft received no dividends for those years. What type of stock did each shareholder own?

_____

_____

_____

10. The United Federated Loan Company, Inc., loaned $10,000 to Grant. Grant secured the loan with a mortgage on his home. His home was later condemned and destroyed by the county. The loan company received no notice before the demolition and consequently sued the city. What legal principle allowed the loan company to sue the county?

_____

_____

_____

38 Corporate Management and Shareholder Control

Chapter Outline

38-1 Management of the Corporation

A. The board of directors has the responsibility to _____

_____

B. The job of the officers of the corporation is to _____

_____

38-2 Management Responsibilities

A. The business judgment rule protects managers who act

   1. _____

   2. _____

   3. _____

   4. _____

B. The fairness rule requires managers to _____

_____

38-3 Shareholder Control

A. Managerial control is _____

_____

B. Corporate democracy is _____

C. Shareholder voting control involves the following:

   1. Cumulative voting allows _____

   _____

   2. A proxy is _____

   3. A voting trust is _____

   _____

   4. A pooling agreement is _____

   _____

   5. A shareholder proposal is _____

D. Shareholder suits consist of the following:

   1. A direct suit is _____

   _____

   2. A derivative suit allows _____

   _____

Other shareholder rights include the following:

A. _____

B. _____

C. _____

D. _____

E. _____

Legal Concepts

For each statement, write T *in the answer column if the statement is true or* F *if the statement is false.*

Answer

1. The business affairs of a corporation are managed by a board of directors that is elected by the shareholders.

1. _T_____

2. Most states prohibit aliens, minors, and nonshareholders from becoming corporate directors.

2. _____

3. Once elected, a director cannot resign from the board.

3. _____

4. Directors must be notified of all regular board meetings.

4. _____

5. Officers have the authority of general agents for the operation of the normal business of the corporation.

5. _____

6. The business judgment rule is one way to encourage people to become corporate managers.

6. _____

7. The fairness rule automatically declares managers to be disloyal if they profit from a corporate decision.

7. _F_____

8. Corporate managers act unfairly if they use inside information to cheat the corporation but not if they use the information to take advantage of corporate outsiders.

8. _____

9. Under the corporate opportunity rule, corporate managers can take a business opportunity for themselves if they first offer it to the corporation and the corporation rejects it.

9. _T_____

10. Cumulative voting is designed to allow minority shareholders an opportunity to be represented on the board of directors.

10. _____

11. Only majority shareholders are allowed to solicit proxies.

11. _____

12. Generally, pooling agreements are interpreted by the court under principles of contract law.

12. _____

13. Before bringing a direct suit against corporate management, shareholders must first exhaust internal remedies.

13. _____

14. Loss of a stock certificate will take away the owner's title to the shares of stock represented by the certificate.

14. _____

15. Once declared, dividends become a debt of the corporation and enforceable by law.

15. _____

Language of the Law

Select the legal term that best matches each definition.

a. business judgment rule
b. corporate democracy
c. corporate opportunity rule
d. cumulative voting
e. derivative suit
f. direct suit

g. fairness rule
h. insider trading
i. managerial control
j. pooling agreement
k. preemptive rights

l. proxy
m. rule of contemporary ownership
n. shareholder proposal
o. voting trust

Answer

1. The ability of one shareholder to cast another shareholder's votes

1. _L_____

2. An agreement among shareholders to transfer their voting rights to a trustee

2. _O_____

3. A suit brought by shareholders who have been deprived of a right that belongs to them as shareholders

4. A shareholder's right to purchase a proportionate share of every new offering of stock by the corporation

5. A theory that holds that managers should be more responsive to shareholders

6. A system of voting that allows shareholders to multiply the number of their voting shares by the number of directors to be elected

7. The rule that holds that in order to institute certain types of lawsuits, shareholders must own stock at the time of the injury and at the time of the suit

8. A suit that allows a shareholder to sue corporate management on behalf of the corporation because of an injury to the corporation

9. The rule that holds that corporate managers cannot take a business opportunity for themselves if they know the corporation would be interested in that same opportunity

10. A suggestion about a broad company policy or procedure that is submitted by a shareholder

3. _____ F

4. _____ K

5. _____ B

6. _____ D

7. _____ m

8. _____ E

9. _____ C

10. _____ N

Applying the Law

1. Burr was a director on the board of the United Satellite Sales and Service Company. He received no notice of a regularly scheduled board meeting to be held on May 2. At the meeting, a majority of the board voted on several proposals that Burr was opposed to. When he heard about the results of the meeting, he argued that all the actions taken were void because he had received no notice of the meeting. Was Burr correct? Explain.

_____

_____

2. Brickley was chairman of the board and chief executive officer of Adario Industries, Inc. On March 3, several hundred acres of prime timberland, owned by Brinkerhoff, Inc., went on the market. After careful examination of the land and a detailed study of the corporation's need for the extra acreage, Brickley decided to buy it. The land proved to be less profitable than Brickley had predicted. Name and explain the rule that would protect Brickley should a shareholder question the decision.

_____

_____

3. Chilcote was the chief executive officer of Royalwood Aircraft, Inc. The company was in the market for a new warehouse. Chilcote sold his own warehouse to Royalwood without revealing his ownership of the building to the board of directors. He also charged Royalwood twice the market value of the warehouse. Identify and explain the rule that will be used to judge Chilcote's behavior.

_____

_____

4. As president of Halvax Construction, Inc., Dunkin knew that Halvax was about to be purchased by Axtel Industries. The purchase would raise the value of Halvax stock by 50 percent. Before the sale and without revealing his knowledge of the impending purchase, Dunkin purchased several hundred shares of Halvax. Identify and explain the rule that will be used to judge Dunkin's conduct.

_____

_____

5. In his role as vice-president of the Brookwood Petroleum Corporation, Finnegan learned that several hundred acres of beachfront property were about to go on sale. Finnegan knew that this was the same property Brookwood had been interested in purchasing last year. Finnegan purchased the property himself and then resold it to the corporation, receiving enormous personal profit. Identify and explain the rule that will be used to judge Finnegan's conduct.

_____

_____

_____

6. As a state senator, Harding had proposed a bill in the state legislature that would guarantee minority shareholders a representative on the board of directors in all corporations incorporated in the state. Identify and explain the theory of corporate management that Harding would support.

_____

_____

_____

7. Dittrich, Beal, and Albright were shareholders in Comstock Assemblies, Inc. They orally created a secret voting trust transferring voting rights to Stanley, who agreed to act as trustee. When Beal changed his mind and pulled out of the voting trust, Dittrich and Albright argued that he had no right to break up the trust. Were they correct? Explain.

_____

_____

_____

8. Pollard owned 5 percent of the voting stock of Roanoke Telespectrum Industries, Inc. The market value of his stock was $900. Sixty days before the next shareholders' meeting, Pollard submitted a 750-word shareholder proposal to the directors of Roanoke Telespectrum. The directors rightfully rejected the proposal. Why?

_____

_____

_____

9. Stowe owned several hundred shares of voting stock in the Volk-Studer Cosmetics Corporation. The directors of Volk-Studer declared that dividends would be paid in the first quarter of the following year. When Stowe did not receive her dividends, she filed suit against the directors of Volk-Studer. The directors told her she could not bring suit because she had not exhausted internal remedies first. Were the directors correct? Explain.

_____

_____

_____

10. Higgins owned 200 shares of Kendall Communications, Inc. Kendall had 600 shares total. Kendall decided to increase its capital stock to 1,200 shares. Assuming that Higgins elected to exercise his preemptive rights, to how many shares would he be entitled?

_____

_____

_____

39 Government Regulation of Corporate Business

Chapter Outline

39-1 Business and the Constitution

A. The regulatory activities of state governments are based on _____

_____

B. The power of the federal government to regulate business is noted in _____

_____

39-2 Securities Regulation

A. The Securities Act of 1933 regulates _____

_____

B. The Securities Exchange Act of 1934 established _____

_____

39-3 Antitrust Regulation

A. The Sherman Anti-Trust Act prohibits _____

_____

B. The Clayton Act polices _____

_____

C. The Robinson-Patman Act deals with _____

_____

D. The Federal Trade Commission Act established _____

_____

39-4 Regulation of Corporate Expansion

A. A merger is _____

_____

B. An asset acquisition is _____

_____

C. A stock acquisition is _____

_____

D. Horizontal expansion occurs _____

_____

E. Vertical expansion occurs _____

_____

F. Conglomerate expansion is _____

_____

39-5 Other Forms of Regulation

A. The Federal Energy Regulatory Commission is _____

_____

B. The Environmental Protection Agency is _____

_____

A. A *quo warranto* action is _____
_____

B. A corporation can be dissolved voluntarily by _____
_____

Legal Concepts

For each statement, write T *in the answer column if the statement is true or* F *if the statement is false.*

Answer

1. The regulatory activities of the federal government are based on its police power.   1. _____
2. The Securities and Exchange Commission (SEC) was established by the Securities Act of 1933.   2. *F*
3. A prospectus is actually a condensed version of a registration statement.   3. _____
4. Agreements between competitors to divide territories among themselves to minimize competition would be lawful if the agreements help the parties compete against others outside the agreement.   4. _____
5. The Clayton Act outlawed tying agreements but legalized interlocking directorates.   5. *F*
6. The Robinson-Patman Act deals with product pricing, advertising, and promotional allowances.   6. _____
7. The SEC is concerned with regulating the expansion of corporations, while the Federal Trade Commission (FTC) is more concerned with the effects of the expansion.   7. _____
8. Today, most legal scholars make no distinction between merger and consolidation.   8. _____
9. In an asset acquisition, the debts of the acquired corporation become liabilities of the acquiring corporation.   9. _____
10. In a stock acquisition, the acquiring corporation deals directly with the shareholders.   10. _____
11. Horizontal mergers are more likely to result in monopolies.   11. _____
12. The Hart-Scott-Rodino Act was designed to police expansion techniques that might harm competition in the marketplace.   12. _____
13. The Environmental Protection Agency is responsible for licensing nuclear power plants.   13. _____
14. If a corporation has repeatedly conducted business in an unlawful manner, the courts can bring a *quo warranto* action against the corporation.   14. _____
15. The government must be informed when a corporation voluntarily dissolves.   15. _____

Language of the Law

Select the legal term that best matches each definition.

a. asset acquisition   f. monopoly   k. suitor
b. conglomerate expansion   g. prospectus   l. takeover
c. consolidation   h. registration statement   m. target
d. horizontal expansion   i. rule-of-reason standard   n. tying agreement
e. merger   j. security   o. vertical expansion

Answer

1. An expansion involving companies that were once in a customer-supplier relationship   1. _____
2. A document that contains detailed information about a corporation, including data about its management, capitalization, and financial condition   2. _____
3. The exclusive control of a market by a business enterprise   3. _____
4. Investment that expects a return solely due to another's effort   4. _____
5. A transaction in which a seller refuses to sell a given product unless the buyer agrees to buy another product from the seller that is related to the first product   5. *N*

6. The purchase of enough voting stock to control a target corporation

7. An expansion involving two companies that were not previously in competition with one another

8. A standard that stops certain practices only if they are an unreasonable restriction of competition

9. A corporate expansion technique that involves one corporation purchasing all of the property of another corporation

10. A corporation that offers to buy the voting stock of another corporation

6. _____

7. _____

8. _____

9. _____

10. _____

Applying the Law

1. Roth owned Images and Illusions, Inc., a fashion-design business that specialized in clothing for the very rich. Roth had four of her richest clients sponsor each of her seasonal lines of clothing. Each contributed $1 million and received a return on that contribution based on Roth's profits each year. Roth claimed that this was not a security. Was she correct? Explain.

_____

_____

2. Holley, a shareholder in Mark One, Inc., was dissatisfied with a decision by Mark One's board's refusing to transfer all of its funds from the Newman National Bank to the Maxcorp City Bank. Since Holley did not own enough stock of his own to gain control of the corporation and reverse the decision, he decided to enter a proxy solicitation campaign. When Holley compiled his proxy solicitation material, he mentioned his controlling interest in Maxcorp by placing it in fine print on the last page of the document. The directors of Mark One filed suit to prevent Holley's campaign from going forward. Holley lost the suit. Why?

_____

_____

3. Oslo Enterprises, Inc., and the Karnes Corporation were the two major mail-order houses in the Midwest. To minimize competition, they negotiated an agreement whereby Oslo would handle all the business in Ohio, Michigan, Wisconsin, and Indiana, and Karnes would handle all the business in Minnesota, Iowa, Missouri, and Illinois. Before the agreement was finalized, corporate counsel for Oslo warned that the agreement would violate federal antitrust laws. The attorney for Karnes argued that the agreement would stand because it was reasonable protection against the east-west mail-order houses. Was the attorney for Karnes correct? Explain.

_____

_____

4. Tolliver Floor Care, Inc., manufactured a line of vacuum cleaners which the Varnes Tile Company wanted to market. Tolliver refused to sell the vacuum cleaner to Varnes unless Varnes also agreed to market Tolliver's floor waxers. Varnes properly objected to the stipulation. Explain.

_____

_____

5. Strickland, a shareholder in Maxwell Dental Supplies, Inc., objected to the corporation's recent asset acquisition of Crown Dental Equipment, Inc. Strickland argued that the asset acquisition was invalid because the directors had not obtained permission from Maxwell's stockholders. Was Strickland correct? Explain.

_____

_____

6. Schuler wanted to purchase Coleman-Walters, Inc. When he approached the board of directors about a merger, they told him they were not interested. Schuler then suggested an asset acquisition. Again the board refused. What measure could Schuler take to sidestep the board of directors in order to obtain control of Coleman-Walters?

_____

_____

_____

7. Refer back to the previous question and consider these additional facts: Schuler elected to follow the alternative means of acquiring Coleman-Walters and the board of directors intended to fight him. What tactic could the board use to fight Schuler's actions?

_____

_____

_____

8. Remy Industries, Inc., purchased all the assets of the Renaissance Landscape Corporation. Remy then proceeded to sell some of those assets while retaining others. The Saunders Nursery claimed that Renaissance owed the nursery several thousand dollars. When Saunders discovered that Remy had purchased the assets of Renaissance, Saunders attempted to recover the debt from Remy. Saunders was unsuccessful. Why?

_____

_____

_____

9. The Dunlap-Winston Petroleum Corporation purchased a storage facility on the banks of the Monongahela River. After filling the storage tanks on the river with crude oil, Dunlap-Winston discovered several structural weaknesses in the tanks. Before the company could act, several thousand gallons of crude oil spilled into the river. The United States sued Dunlap-Winston for violating federal pollution laws. Dunlap-Winston argued that it should not be liable because the pollution was unintentional. Was Dunlap-Winston correct? Explain.

_____

_____

_____

10. Yetzer Delivery Service, Inc., was properly incorporated under the appropriate state statute. Nevertheless, Yetzer had not paid any franchise taxes nor had the corporation filed annual reports. Yetzer had also failed to maintain a registered agent for service of process as is required by state law. What could the state do about this situation?

_____

_____

_____

40 Professional Liability

Chapter Outline

40-1 The Liability of Accountants

A. An accountant is _____

_____

B. Generally accepted accounting principles outline _____

C. Generally accepted auditing standards measure _____

D. An accountant might be liable to clients under common law for

1. _____

2. _____

E. Accountants can be held liable for violating the following statutes

1. _____

2. _____

3. _____

40-2 The Liability of Other Business Professionals

A. An architect is _____

_____

1. The architects' standard of care requires that _____

_____

2. The cost of repair rule holds that _____

_____

B. An attorney is _____

_____

1. An attorney has the duty to represent his or her clients with

a. _____

b. _____

c. _____

2. Attorneys are rarely held liable to third parties because _____

_____

40-3 The Liability of Health Care Providers

A. Health care providers are _____

_____

B. Health care providers are regulated by the state and _____

_____

C. Determining how the reasonable health care provider would act in a given situation can be determined by reference to

1. _____

2. _____

3. _____

Legal Concepts

For each statement, write T *in the answer column if the statement is true or* F *if the statement is false.*

Answer

1. The only job of an accountant is to keep financial records for his or her clients.   1. _____
2. The state cannot prevent someone from practicing accounting as a profession.   2. _____
3. An auditor is a guarantor of an institution's financial records.   3. _____
4. Auditing standards explain how an auditor can determine whether proper accounting procedures have been used.   4. _____
5. According to the accounting profession's Code of Professional Ethics, an accountant cannot reveal information about a client's business to anyone, even when ordered to do so by a court of law.   5. _____
6. An accountant can never be held liable to third parties who might be damaged by a negligently prepared financial statement.   6. _____
7. Accountants cannot be found liable for violating state blue sky laws.   7. _____
8. Under its police power, the state can regulate the conduct of architects.   8. _____
9. The standard of care requires an architect to use the same methods, techniques, and procedures that an architect of ordinary skill would use in a similar situation.   9. _____
10. Architects, like all other professionals, are held liable for all mistakes made while on the job.   10. _____
11. Attorneys must have one year of on-the-job experience before they can practice law.   11. _____
12. If an attorney fails to act in the best interests of a client, the attorney faces a potential lawsuit brought by the client and potential disciplinary action brought by the state.   12. _____
13. An attorney can represent two clients on opposite sides of the same dispute as long as both sides consent to the dual representation.   13. _____
14. Informed consent must be in writing on a form signed by the patient and witnessed by a third party.   14. _____
15. Determining how a reasonable health care professional would act in a given situation can be decided only by reference to the policy or procedure manual.   15. _____

Language of the Law

Select the legal term that best matches each definition.

a. adverse opinion
b. audit
c. certified public accountant (CPA)
d. Code of Professional Ethics
e. disclaimer

f. general consent
g. generally accepted accounting principles (GAAP)
h. generally accepted auditing standards (GAAS)
i. informed consent

j. national standard
k. professional
l. public accountant (PA)
m. qualified opinion
n. similar locality rule
o. unqualified opinion

Answer

1. An accountant who has met certain age, character, education, experience, and testing requirements   1. _____
2. Rules that outline the procedures that accountants must use in accumulating financial data and in preparing financial statements   2. _____

3. An opinion issued by an auditor that concludes that the records of a company are an accurate reflection of the company's financial status

        3. _____

4. An individual who can perform a highly specialized task because of his or her special abilities, education, experience, and knowledge

        4. _____

5. An examination of the financial records of an organization to determine whether those records are a fair presentation of the actual financial health of the organization

        5. _____

6. A declaration that states that an auditor has decided not to give any opinion on a company's financial records

        6. _____

7. Written consent that must be obtained when a diagnostic test administered to a patient will be dangerous or painful

        7. _____

8. An opinion issued by an auditor when the financial statements do not fairly represent the financial health of the organization

        8. _____

9. The rule that compares rural hospitals to rural hospitals, urban hospitals to urban hospitals, and suburban hospitals to suburban hospitals when determining the liability of a health care provider

        9. _____

10. Consent given the moment a patient enters a hospital setting

       10. _____

Applying the Law

1. Webber was neither a CPA nor a PA. Despite this fact, she opened an office and advertised that she would perform bookkeeping services at reasonable rates. Banner told Webber that she could not provide such services without first becoming either a CPA or a PA. Why was Banner's statement inaccurate?

_____

_____

2. Ackerman was hired to audit the books of the Baumann Corporation. When he was finished with his work, Ackerman issued an opinion that stated that the books represented the company's health as of the date of the completion of the audit. Ackerman added that a lawsuit pending against Baumann could affect the company's health. Identify the type of opinion that Ackerman issued in this case.

_____

_____

3. Baird was hired to audit the books of the Hatch Company. After completing her work, Baird issued an opinion that said that the Hatch Company bookkeeper had consistently ignored generally accepted accounting principles and had failed to disclose some very important financial information. What kind of an opinion had Baird issued?

_____

_____

4. Gibson was hired by Houston to prepare a financial statement about Houston's business. Houston told Gibson that he wanted the financial statement to convince McCoy to invest in his business. Gibson made several crucial errors in the statement because he failed to use the same skill and competence that a reasonable accounting professional would use in a similar situation. McCoy relied on the statement and lost a great deal of money as a result. Why would Gibson be liable to McCoy even though McCoy was not his client?

_____

_____

_____

5. Jameson was the regular accountant for Lakeview Industries, Inc. Noll, the president of Lakeview, asked Jameson to develop an extra set of financial records that would indicate that Lakeview was much healthier than it actually was. Jameson did as Noll asked. Metcalf, an investor, was misled by the information and lost a great deal of money. When Metcalf named Jameson in a lawsuit, Jameson argued that since Metcalf was not a client or a named third party, she could not bring the suit against him. Was Jameson correct? Explain.

_____

_____

6. Podmore was the architect who had worked on plans for the new Monroe City Library. Podmore had made several mistakes in calculating how much weight a balcony in the library could hold. Jefferson, the contractor, ignored Podmore's plans and made his own calculations, which also proved to be incorrect. When the books were moved onto the balcony, it collapsed under the weight. Podmore argued that she should not be held liable. Was she correct? Explain.

_____

_____

7. Renkar, an attorney, was hired by Stover to act as his agent as he negotiated a new contract with the Cutler City Comets, a professional soccer team. Unknown to Stover, Renkar was also on the board of directors of the Cutler City Comets. What duty did Renkar violate in this situation?

_____

_____

8. Zent acted as York's attorney in York's suit against his former employer, the Albert Restaurant Chain of America, Inc. York was fighting a contractual clause that would have prevented him from working as a chef for any of Albert's competitors for two years. When York won the case, Albert sued Zent for helping York in his fight to retain his position as chef for the Carmine Restaurant Chain. Albert's suit failed. Explain.

_____

_____

9. Passarelli entered Cumberland County General Hospital for several diagnostic X rays. Before taking the X rays, Dr. DeLong had to inject Passerelli with a contrast medium. To save time and trouble, DeLong told Passarelli that the consent form was an insurance form. When Passarelli had an adverse reaction to the contrast medium, he sued DeLong and the hospital for battery. Why won't the consent form protect DeLong or the hospital?

_____

_____

10. Brodsky was a patient at Shields Memorial Hospital, Quinn was a nurse at Shields. While Brodsky was out of the room, Quinn accidentally spilled a pitcher of water on the floor of Brodsky's room. Before cleaning up the mess, Quinn took her lunch break. When Brodsky returned to his room, he slipped in the puddle of water, fell, and injured himself. Brodsky sued Quinn and the hospital for negligence. At the trial, Brodsky argued that there was no need for an expert witness to testify as to the standards of care rendered by the nurse. Was Brodsky correct? Explain.

_____

_____

_____

41 Computer Law

Chapter Outline

41-1 The Law and the Computer

  A. Computer hardware refers to _____

  B. Computer software refers to _____

  C. A computer program is _____

41-2 The Ownership of a Computer Program

  A. A trade secret is _____

    1. Trade secret status is unavailable to _____

    _____

    2. Trade secret status is available to _____

    _____

  B. A patent is _____

    1. A computer program is ineligible for patent protection when _____

    _____

    2. A computer program is eligible for patent protection when _____

    _____

  C. A copyright is _____

    1. It is not copyright infringement to _____

    2. It is copyright infringement to _____

41-3 Contract Law and the Computer

  A. A contract for the sale of a computer itself is a _____ contract.

  B. A software package is usually considered to be a _____ contract.

  C. When computer hardware and computer software are sold as a combination, the sale is considered to be a _____ contract.

  D. Customized program contracts are considered to be _____ contracts.

41-4 Privacy Law and the Computer

  A. Computers can be used to violate the two freedoms that arise from the right of privacy in tort law. The freedoms are

    1. _____

    2. _____

  B. Computers can be used to violate the right to privacy implied by several provisions in the U.S. Constitution, including

    1. _____

    2. _____

41-5 Crime and the Computer

  A. Computer trespass is _____

  B. Computer fraud is _____

  C. Computer-related crimes include _____

  _____

D. Two prominent federal statutes that specifically target computer-related crimes are

1. _____

2. _____

Legal Concepts

For each statement, write T *in the answer column if the statement is true or* F *if the statement is false.*

Answer

1. Computer law has developed by borrowing principles from contract law, tort law, criminal law, and property law.

    1. _____

2. Computer programs that have been transferred to software and then placed on the open market for wide distribution cannot claim trade secret status.

    2. _____

3. Computer programs that stand alone are eligible for patent protection if they are based on mathematical formulas.

    3. _____

4. Copyright protection does not extend to the type of visual display produced by a computer.

    4. _____

5. The purchase of a keyboard, terminal, disk drive, and printer would be a sale-of-goods contract.

    5. _____

6. The hiring of an individual programmer to create a unique program designed for one customer is considered to be a service contract.

    6. _____

7. The constitutional right to privacy applies to both the government and to nongovernmental parties.

    7. _____

8. The Fair Credit Reporting Act prohibits credit bureaus from revealing an individual's credit history to an insurance company or a bank without an official court order.

    8. _____

9. Trade secret status is available to companies that distribute their software on a limited, highly selective basis.

    9. _____

10. The legal validity of box-top licensing is no longer in question.

    10. _____

11. Under copyright law, it is not an infringement for the owner of software to copy it if the duplication is essential in the use of a particular computer.

    11. _____

12. Most states have found it difficult to designate computer hardware and software as property that can be stolen.

    12. _____

13. Computer fraud includes adding or deleting a computer program or data, but does not include altering that program or data.

    13. _____

14. Federal laws prohibiting mail fraud and wire fraud have been used to prosecute computer criminals.

    14. _____

15. The Counterfeit Access Device and Computer Fraud and Abuse Act applies only to computers involved in national defense.

    15. _____

Language of the Law

Select the legal term that best matches each definition.

a. box-top license
b. computer fraud
c. computer package
d. computer program
e. computer trespass
f. device
g. federal interest computer
h. hardware
i. intellectual property
j. licensing agreement
k. mail fraud
l. software
m. substantial similarity test
n. trade secret
o. wire fraud

Answer

1. A transaction by which the producer of a computer program allows a purchaser to use the program only if the purchaser agrees to respect the producer's desire for secrecy

    1. _____

2. An agreement on a software box that limits the buyer's right to copy the program, to reveal the contents of the program, or to allow others to use the program   2. _____

3. The actual device known as a computer and its components   3. _____

4. The card, tape, disk, or silicon chip that contains a computer program   4. _____

5. Instructions that tell computer hardware what to do and when to do it   5. _____

6. A plan, process, or device used in a business and known only to employees who need to know about it to carry out their jobs   6. _____

7. A computer used only by the government or by a financial institution   7. _____

8. Obtaining money, property, or services through the fraudulent use of a computer   8. _____

9. Data, programs, software, computer material, and any confidential information in any form that is stored in or used by a computer   9. _____

10. Gaining access to a computer with the intent to commit a crime   10. _____

Applying the Law

1. The Bradley Electronics Corporation developed a new computer program that would help consumers prepare their tax returns under the new federal income tax law. The program was marketed for wide distribution in a software package labeled "Taxes 'R Fun." Explain why Bradley Electronics would not be able to claim that their new product is a trade secret.

_____

_____

2. Product design engineers at Nutech Concepts, Inc., developed a new process for destroying certain types of dangerous chemical pollutants. Part of the process had to be controlled by a computer, following the directions of a computer program. This part of the process was only about 20 percent of the entire operation. The patent examiner denied Nutech's request for a patent on the process. A federal court reversed the refusal. Why?

_____

_____

3. Jefferson developed a computer program that allowed instructors to input student test results into a computer. The program allowed the computer to store the students' results and figure out their final grades. Essentially, the program allowed the computer to serve as a memory aid and calculator for the instructor. The patent office correctly refused to grant Jefferson's patent. Why?

_____

_____

4. Davis copied the program of a video game known as AIRCARRIER. To make his copy appear different, he changed the video display, altered the speed of the game, and renamed the game CARRIER WAR. The owners of AIRCARRIER sued Davis for copyright infringement. Davis argued that no infringement had occurred because his visual display was different from the visual display of AIRCARRIER. Was Davis correct? Explain.

_____

_____

_____

_____

5. Micrographics, Inc., developed and sold a software package called MARKET MANAGEMENT. The software package allowed consumers to use their home computers to keep track of financial investments. Underwood wrote a brand-new program but reproduced exactly the visual display of MARKET MANAGEMENT. He sold his software package under the name FINANCIAL MANAGEMENT. Micrographics sued Underwood for copyright infringement. Underwood defended his actions by pointing out that he had written his own program to produce FINANCIAL MANAGEMENT. Underwood's defense failed. Why?

_____

_____

6. Lee purchased a software package from the Hilliard Book Store. The software was supposed to help consumers learn how to play chess. When the software package failed to work properly, Lee returned it to Hilliard. The manager of Hilliard argued that the software sale was not covered by any Uniform Commercial Code (UCC) warranties because it was a service contract rather than a sale-of-goods contract. Was the manager correct? Explain.

_____

_____

7. The Monroe Tire Company purchased a computer from Computrol Industries, Inc. The computer was supposed to perform multiple functions for Monroe, including the management of payroll, the keeping of inventory records, the computation of accounts receivable, and the payment of bills. As part of the contract, Computrol agreed to program the system for Monroe. After a half year of frustrating attempts to get the computer on-line, technicians from Computrol could not make the computer operational. The only function available was payroll management. Monroe demanded removal of the computer and a return of the money paid for it. Computrol argued that the contract was a service contract and could not be rescinded. Was Computrol wrong? Explain.

_____

_____

8. Martin Investigations, Inc., a private security operation, was hired by Lewis Enterprises to do a background check on Cirocco as part of its hiring process. When Cirocco found out that Martin and Lewis had compiled a computerized record on her, she claimed her constitutional right of privacy had been violated. Was she correct? Explain.

_____

_____

9. Crosby found out from a friend that the Troyville Credit Bureau had passed on several inaccurate credit reports to three banks, all of which had refused to give Crosby a loan. Crosby went to the credit bureau but was told that he could not see what was in his file. Crosby argued that he had a right to see his credit information. Was Crosby correct in his argument? Explain.

_____

_____

10. Jenkins was director of the computer department at Wheatley Union College. Jenkins altered computer records to allow his friends to go to classes without having to pay tuition and he was prosecuted for violating a state law prohibiting computer fraud. He defended his actions by pointing out that he'd stolen neither money nor property from Wheatley. Jenkins's defense failed. Explain.

_____

_____

Key

Chapter 1

Legal Concepts

1. T	6. F	11. T
2. F	7. T	12. F
3. F	8. F	13. F
4. F	9. T	14. F
5. T	10. T	15. F

Language of the Law

1. g	6. i
2. l	7. m
3. j	8. b
4. e	9. o
5. c	10. a

Chapter 2

Legal Concepts

1. F	6. F	11. F
2. F	7. T	12. F
3. F	8. T	13. T
4. T	9. T	14. T
5. T	10. F	15. T

Language of the Law

1. k	6. b
2. j	7. i
3. d	8. h
4. e	9. f
5. g	10. a

Chapter 3

Legal Concepts

1. T	6. T	11. T
2. F	7. F	12. F
3. F	8. T	13. T
4. F	9. F	14. F
5. T	10. T	15. T

Language of the Law

1. i	6. k
2. g	7. h
3. n	8. m
4. b	9. e
5. j	10. o

Chapter 4

Legal Concepts

1. T	6. F	11. F
2. F	7. T	12. T
3. F	8. F	13. T
4. F	9. T	14. T
5. F	10. T	15. F

Language of the Law

1. d	6. f
2. g	7. h
3. i	8. e
4. j	9. a
5. k	10. c

Chapter 5

Legal Concepts

1. T	6. F	11. F
2. T	7. T	12. T
3. F	8. F	13. T
4. F	9. F	14. F
5. F	10. T	15. F

Language of the Law

1. l	6. g
2. a	7. e
3. j	8. i
4. b	9. f
5. h	10. c

Chapter 6

Legal Concepts

1. F	6. F	11. T
2. F	7. T	12. T
3. T	8. F	13. F
4. T	9. F	14. T
5. T	10. T	15. F

Language of the Law

1. d	6. e
2. i	7. m
3. f	8. a
4. c	9. b
5. j	10. n

Chapter 7

Legal Concepts

1. T	6. F	11. T
2. F	7. F	12. T
3. F	8. F	13. F
4. T	9. T	14. T
5. F	10. T	15. F

Language of the Law

1. j	6. e
2. g	7. f
3. c	8. o
4. k	9. l
5. h	10. i

Chapter 8

Legal Concepts

1. T	6. T	11. F
2. T	7. F	12. T
3. T	8. T	13. F
4. F	9. F	14. F
5. F	10. T	15. T

Language of the Law

1. a	6. i
2. n	7. b
3. g	8. k
4. h	9. m
5. c	10. o

Chapter 9

Legal Concepts

1. T	6. T	11. F
2. F	7. T	12. T
3. T	8. F	13. T
4. T	9. F	14. F
5. F	10. T	15. T

Language of the Law

1. f	6. d
2. o	7. h
3. l	8. g
4. e	9. b and m
5. c	10. k

Chapter 10

Legal Concepts

1. T	6. F	11. T
2. T	7. T	12. T
3. T	8. F	13. F
4. T	9. F	14. F
5. F	10. F	15. F

Language of the Law

1. h	6. a
2. n	7. k
3. i	8. g
4. m	9. j
5. e	10. d

Chapter 11

Legal Concepts

1. T	6. T	11. T
2. F	7. T	12. T
3. F	8. T	13. T
4. F	9. F	14. T
5. F	10. T	15. F

Language of the Law

1. c	6. e
2. g	7. d
3. k	8. a
4. l	9. j
5. m	10. n

Chapter 12

Legal Concepts

1. F	6. F	11. T
2. T	7. T	12. F
3. F	8. T	13. T
4. F	9. T	14. T
5. T	10. F	15. F

Language of the Law

1. k	6. o
2. j	7. g
3. b	8. i
4. c	9. l
5. a	10. n

Chapter 13

Legal Concepts

1. T	6. F	11. F
2. F	7. T	12. T
3. F	8. T	13. F
4. T	9. T	14. F
5. T	10. F	15. T

Language of the Law

1. i	6. h
2. g	7. c
3. b	8. d
4. l	9. k
5. f	10. o

Chapter 14

Legal Concepts

1. T	6. F	11. F
2. F	7. F	12. T
3. F	8. T	13. T
4. T	9. F	14. T
5. F	10. T	15. F

Language of the Law

1. k	6. i
2. c	7. m
3. l	8. j
4. a	9. n
5. d	10. h

Chapter 15

Legal Concepts

1. T	6. F	11. T
2. F	7. F	12. F
3. T	8. T	13. T
4. T	9. T	14. F
5. F	10. F	15. T

Language of the Law

1. e	6. h
2. c	7. m
3. g	8. l
4. k	9. n
5. a	10. f

Chapter 16

Legal Concepts

1. T	6. F	11. T
2. F	7. F	12. F
3. F	8. T	13. F
4. T	9. T	14. T
5. T	10. T	15. T

Language of the Law

1. d	6. e
2. j	7. n
3. c	8. g
4. f	9. l
5. o	10. i

Chapter 17

Legal Concepts

1. T	6. F	11. T
2. T	7. F	12. F
3. F	8. T	13. T
4. T	9. T	14. T
5. F	10. F	15. F

Language of the Law

1. f	6. c
2. d	7. a
3. h	8. j
4. g	9. n
5. o	10. m

Chapter 18

Legal Concepts

1. F	6. F	11. F
2. F	7. F	12. F
3. T	8. T	13. F
4. T	9. T	14. T
5. T	10. T	15. T

Language of the Law

1. d	6. g
2. m	7. i
3. n	8. l
4. k	9. o
5. c	10. j

Chapter 19
Legal Concepts

1. F	6. F	11. F
2. T	7. F	12. T
3. F	8. F	13. F
4. T	9. T	14. F
5. T	10. F	15. T

Language of the Law

1. b	6. j
2. i	7. d
3. n	8. e
4. g	9. k
5. h	10. a

Chapter 20
Legal Concepts

1. F	6. F	11. F
2. F	7. F	12. F
3. T	8. T	13. T
4. F	9. T	14. F
5. T	10. T	15. T

Language of the Law

1. b	6. j
2. o	7. n
3. h	8. i
4. l	9. f
5. e	10. m

Chapter 21
Legal Concepts

1. T	6. F	11. F
2. F	7. F	12. T
3. F	8. T	13. T
4. T	9. T	14. F
5. T	10. T	15. T

Language of the Law

1. k	6. f
2. l	7. m
3. h	8. o
4. e	9. d
5. a	10. n

Chapter 22
Legal Concepts

1. F	6. T	11. F
2. T	7. T	12. F
3. T	8. F	13. T
4. F	9. F	14. T
5. F	10. T	15. T

Language of the Law

1. i	6. d
2. o	7. m
3. e	8. c
4. j	9. h
5. k	10. f

Chapter 23
Legal Concepts

1. T	6. F	11. F
2. F	7. F	12. F
3. F	8. T	13. T
4. T	9. T	14. F
5. F	10. T	15. T

Language of the Law

1. e	6. g
2. a	7. o
3. j	8. i
4. l	9. m
5. k	10. d

Chapter 24
Legal Concepts

1. F	6. F	11. T
2. F	7. F	12. T
3. T	8. T	13. F
4. F	9. F	14. F
5. T	10. T	15. T

Language of the Law

1. l	6. e
2. a	7. m
3. j	8. b
4. d	9. i
5. h	10. n

Chapter 25

Legal Concepts

1. T	6. T	11. F
2. T	7. F	12. F
3. F	8. T	13. T
4. F	9. T	14. F
5. T	10. F	15. T

Language of the Law

1. m	6. b
2. a	7. h
3. f	8. l
4. n	9. k
5. g	10. d

Chapter 26

Legal Concepts

1. F	6. T	11. T
2. T	7. T	12. F
3. F	8. F	13. F
4. T	9. T	14. F
5. F	10. T	15. T

Language of the Law

1. n	6. l
2. e	7. b
3. c	8. a
4. g	9. d
5. j	10. f

Chapter 27

Legal Concepts

1. T	6. F	11. T
2. F	7. T	12. T
3. T	8. F	13. T
4. T	9. T	14. F
5. F	10. F	15. F

Language of the Law

1. j	6. g or h
2. n	7. d
3. e	8. m
4. k	9. a
5. f	10. l

Chapter 28

Legal Concepts

1. F	6. T	11. F
2. T	7. F	12. T
3. F	8. F	13. T
4. F	9. T	14. F
5. T	10. T	15. F

Language of the Law

1. i	6. o
2. f	7. l
3. d	8. b
4. g	9. a
5. m	10. n

Chapter 29

Legal Concepts

1. T	6. F	11. F
2. T	7. F	12. T
3. F	8. T	13. T
4. F	9. F	14. T
5. T	10. T	15. F

Language of the Law

1. l	6. m
2. a	7. h
3. g	8. i
4. e	9. d
5. c	10. n

Chapter 30

Legal Concepts

1. T	6. F	11. F
2. F	7. F	12. T
3. F	8. T	13. T
4. T	9. F	14. T
5. F	10. T	15. F

Language of the Law

1. g	6. b
2. a	7. j
3. f	8. c
4. h	9. k
5. n	10. i

Chapter 31

Legal Concepts

1. F	6. T	11. T
2. T	7. T	12. F
3. F	8. F	13. F
4. T	9. T	14. F
5. F	10. F	15. T

Language of the Law

1. k	6. i
2. c	7. l
3. f	8. n
4. b or i	9. e
5. a	10. d

Chapter 32

Legal Concepts

1. F	6. F	11. F
2. T	7. T	12. T
3. T	8. F	13. F
4. F	9. F	14. F
5. F	10. T	15. T

Language of the Law

1. h	6. c
2. g	7. e
3. l	8. b
4. n	9. d
5. a	10. f

Chapter 33

Legal Concepts

1. T	6. T	11. F
2. F	7. F	12. T
3. T	8. T	13. F
4. F	9. T	14. F
5. T	10. F	15. T

Language of the Law

1. f	6. n
2. b	7. l
3. m	8. a
4. c	9. d
5. o	10. j

Chapter 34

Legal Concepts

1. F	6. T	11. F
2. T	7. T	12. F
3. T	8. T	13. F
4. F	9. T	14. F
5. T	10. T	15. F

Language of the Law

1. d	6. k
2. c	7. f
3. i	8. b
4. j	9. g
5. e	10. a

Chapter 35

Legal Concepts

1. T	6. F	11. T
2. F	7. F	12. T
3. F	8. T	13. F
4. F	9. F	14. T
5. T	10. F	15. T

Language of the Law

1. g	6. l
2. f	7. d
3. j	8. h
4. n	9. i
5. m	10. c

Chapter 36

Legal Concepts

1. F	6. T	11. F
2. T	7. F	12. F
3. F	8. T	13. T
4. F	9. F	14. T
5. F	10. T	15. F

Language of the Law

1. g	6. c
2. f	7. b
3. o	8. k
4. n	9. i
5. j	10. a

Chapter 37

Legal Concepts

1. F	6. T	11. F
2. T	7. T	12. F
3. F	8. F	13. F
4. T	9. T	14. T
5. F	10. F	15. T

Language of the Law

1. j	6. f
2. b	7. a
3. c	8. o
4. n	9. l
5. i	10. m

Chapter 38

Legal Concepts

1. T	6. T	11. F
2. F	7. F	12. T
3. F	8. F	13. F
4. F	9. T	14. F
5. T	10. T	15. T

Language of the Law

1. l	6. d
2. o	7. m
3. f	8. e
4. k	9. c
5. b	10. n

Chapter 39

Legal Concepts

1. F	6. T	11. T
2. F	7. T	12. T
3. T	8. T	13. F
4. F	9. F	14. F
5. F	10. T	15. T

Language of the Law

1. o	6. l
2. h	7. b
3. f	8. i
4. j	9. a
5. n	10. k

Chapter 40

Legal Concepts

1. F	6. F	11. F
2. T	7. F	12. T
3. F	8. T	13. T
4. T	9. T	14. T
5. F	10. F	15. F

Language of the Law

1. c	6. e
2. g	7. i
3. o	8. a
4. k	9. n
5. b	10. f

Chapter 41

Legal Concepts

1. T	6. T	11. T
2. T	7. F	12. F
3. F	8. F	13. F
4. F	9. T	14. T
5. T	10. F	15. F

Language of the Law

1. j	6. n
2. a	7. g
3. h	8. b
4. l	9. i
5. d	10. e